LIFE BEHIND BARBED WIRE

WORLD WAR II: THE GLOBAL, HUMAN, AND ETHICAL DIMENSION

G. Kurt Piehler, series editor

LIFE BEHIND BARBED WIRE

THE SECRET WORLD WAR II PHOTOGRAPHS OF PRISONER OF WAR ANGELO M. SPINELLI

Angelo M. Spinelli and Lewis H. Carlson

Fordham University Press   New York   2004

All photos reprinted courtesy of Andersonville National Historic Site, National Park Service, and Angelo Spinelli.

World War II: The Global, Human, and Ethical Dimension, No. 2
ISSN 1541-0293

Library of Congress Cataloging-in-Publication Data

Spinelli, Angelo M.
    Life behind barbed wire : the secret World War II photographs of prisoner of war Angelo M. Spinelli / Angelo M. Spinelli and Lewis H. Carlson.
        p. cm. — (World War II—the global, human, and ethical dimension ; no. 2)
        ISBN 0-8232-2305-1 (alk. paper)
    1. Spinelli, Angelo M. 2. World War, 1939–1945—Prisoners and prisons, German. 3. World War, 1939–1945—Personal narratives, American. 4. Prisoners of war—United States—Biography. 5. Prisoners of war—Germany—Biography. 6. Stalag III B—Pictorial works. 7. Stalag III A—Pictoral works. I. Carlson, Lewis H. II. Title. III. World War II—the global, human, and ethical dimension ; 2.
        D805.5.S717S65 2004
        940.54'7243'092—dc22

                                                                                            2003018410

Designed by Brady McNamara
Printed in the United States of America
08 07 06 05 04   5 4 3 2 1
First edition

Angelo Spinelli dedicates this book to his late wife, Anna Egidio Spinelli, who waited fifty long months for Angelo to return from combat and captivity, and to his late brother, Joe, who sent him many of the cigars and cigarettes that allowed him to trade with guards and other internees in Stalag IIIB. This book is further dedicated to all former prisoners of war, and to those who neither witnessed nor understood the POW experience.

CONTENTS

ACKNOWLEDGMENTS

Primary thanks and gratitude are due Fred Sanchez, Chief of Interpretation and Resource Management of the Andersonville Historic Site, National Park Service, without whose help Angelo Spinelli's extraordinary photographs would have remained largely unknown. Mr. Sanchez initially encouraged Spinelli to donate his entire collection to the National Prisoner of War Museum; then, after expending countless hours improving the quality of the negatives, he successfully found grant money for an April 2000 exhibit titled "Behind the Barbed Wire: Angelo Spinelli's Photo-Documentation on Life and Culture in a POW Stalag Camp." Sponsored by the National Prisoner of War Museum at Andersonville, Georgia, this exhibit, featuring ninety-two Spinelli photographs, traveled the country before finding a permanent home in the Italian American Museum in New York City in the spring of 2003. In addition, Mr. Sanchez helped us prepare the photos for this book.

Special thanks are due Eric Reinert, the former curator at Andersonville Historic Site, to Alan Marsh, Andersonville's Cultural Resources Program Manager, and to POW historian Robert C. Doyle, all of whom gave generously of their time and expertise.

Thanks also to Jack. T. Sneesby, whose unpublished prison memoir provided excellent background descriptions of Stalag IIIB and IIIA and of the forced march that almost killed Angelo Spinelli in February 1945. Thanks as well to Edward La Porta, whose actions on that march unquestionably saved Spinelli's life, and to Burdette Parrott, who lived in Spinelli's barracks, both of whom willingly shared their memories. Very generous with personal papers were Mrs. Norma Varley, who made available her late husband Robert Varley's prison diary, and Dr. Tim Wolter, whose book, *POW Baseball in World War II: The National Pastime Behind Barbed Wire*, features several Spinelli photographs. Finally, we thank family, friends, and, especially, former POWs who have encouraged us to do this book.

THE ANGELO SPINELLI TIME LINE

March 14, 1917	Angelo Spinelli is born in the Bronx, New York.
July 25, 1941	Drafted into the U.S. Army.
November 8, 1942	Lands at Algiers in North Africa with the First Armored Division.
February 14, 1943	Captured by Field Marshal Erwin Rommel's troops during the Battle of Fiad Pass in Tunisia.
March 29, 1943	Arrives in Stalag IIIB at Fürstenberg/Oder.
August 1943	Bribes a guard in Stalag IIIB to procure his first camera.
January 31, 1945	Evacuated from Stalag IIIB because of the advancing Russian Army, and begins the Long March to Stalag IIIA.

February 7, 1945	Arrives in Stalag IIIA at Luckenwalde.
April 22, 1945	Liberated from Stalag IIIA by Russian troops.
June 13, 1945	Arrives back in the United States.
July 23, 1945	Honored by the New York Young Men's Christian Association where he first publicly reveals his photographs.
July 29, 1945	Marries Anna Egidio.
September 21, 1945	Honorably discharged from the U.S. Army.
1946	National Council of YMCAs publishes a thirty-seven-page booklet titled *The Yankee Kriegies*, which features his photographs and the POW paintings of C. Ross Greening.
1981	Time-Life Books publishes fourteen of Spinelli's photographs in its *Prisoners of World War II*, the first public showing of his photos in thirty-five years.
June 5, 2000	Donates more than 400 photographs and negatives to the National POW Museum at Andersonville, Georgia.
April 2003	The traveling exhibit of his "Behind The Barbed Wire" finds a permanent home in the Italian American Museum in New York, N.Y.

Barth
(Stalag Luft 1)

Grosstychow
(Stalag Luft 4)

Marienburg
(Stalag 20-B)

Bremervorde
(Stalag 10-B)

Neubrandenburg
(Stalag 2-A)

Hammerstein
(Stalag 2-B)

Tórun
(Stalag 20-A)

(Oflag 10-B)
Nienburg
(Stalag 10-C)

Fallingbostel
(Stalag 11-B)

Schubin
(Oflag 64)

Orbke
(Stalag 357)

Alt Drewitz
(Stalag 3-C)

Brunswick
(Oflag 11/79)

Altengrabow
(Stalag 11-A)

BERLIN

Fürstenburg
(Stalag 3-B)

Krefeld
(Stalag 6-J)

G E R M A N Y

Steglitz
(Stalag 3-D)

Luckenwalde
(Stalag 3-A)

P O L A N D

Spangenburg
(Oflag 9 A/H)

Annaburg
(Stalag 4-D/Z)

(Stalag Luft 3)
Sagan
(Stalag 8-C)

Bergisch-Neustadt
(Stalag 6-G)

Bad Sulza
(Stalag 9-C)

Torgau
(Stalag 4-D)

Mühlberg
(Stalag 4-B)

Waldbreitbach
(Stalag 12-D)

Rotenburg
(Oflag 9 A/Z)

Oschatz
(Stalag 4-G)

Bankau
(Stalag Luft 7)

Wetzlar
(Dulag Luft)

Colditz (Oflag 4-C)

Hohnstein
(Stalag 4-A)

Lamsdorf
(Stalag 344)

Limburg
(Stalag 12-A)

Bad Orb
(Stalag 9-B)

Hartmannsdorf
(Stalag 4-F)

Hammelburg
(Stalag 13-C)

Wistritz
(Stalag 4-C)

Teschen
(Stalag 8-B)

Freinsheim
(Stalag 12-F)

Nürnberg
(Stalag 13-D)

Weiden
(Stalag 13-B)

C Z E C H O S L O V A K I A

Ludwigsburg
(Stalag 5-A)

Eichstätt
(Oflag 7-B)

Hohenfels
(Stalag 383)

Offenburg
(Stalag 5-C)

Villingen
(Stalag 5-B)

Moosburg
(Stalag 7-A)

Krems
(Stalag 17-B)

Memmingen
(Stalag 7-B)

Pupping
(Stalag 398)

Kaisersteinbruch
(Stalag 17-A)

A U S T R I A

Markt-Pongau
(Stalag 18-C 317)

Wolfsberg
(Stalag 18-A)

For enlisted men or non-commissioned officers
For airmen
For officers
For enlisted men and airmen
For enlisted men and officers

0   50   100
Miles

Major German camps that held Amercan POWs

XIII

INTRODUCTION

Lewis Carlson

*I felt a moral obligation to show how we survived regardless
of hardship. I felt by taking my prison-of-war photos, I'd be
doing a service to my country.*

ANGELO SPINELLI

ON JULY 23, 1945, the Young Men's Christian Association of the
City of New York hosted a "Welcome Home" luncheon at the Hotel
Commodore to honor local sons who had been prisoners of war in Nazi
Germany. Among the thirty-four men so honored was Sgt. Angelo
Spinelli, a twenty-eight-year-old former watchmaker from the Bronx,
who had been a U.S. Army Signal Corps photographer before spending
twenty-six months as a POW. When Spinelli mentioned to YMCA
Director of Public Relations John R. Burkhart that he had used a hid-
den camera to take more than a thousand photographs of life inside a
German prison camp, Buckhart was incredulous, but not for long. After
Spinelli showed him several hundred high-quality photographs,
Burkhart quickly arranged to have a representative sampling published
in a 1946 booklet titled *The Yankee Kriegies*.[1] The YMCA distributed
50,000 copies of *The Yankee Kriegies*, most of them during a traveling
exhibit of Spinelli's photographs and the watercolor paintings of fellow

prisoner C. Ross Greening. Incredibly, this tour would be the last public exposure for Spinelli's magnificent photographs for thirty-five years.

✪

I FIRST ENCOUNTERED Angelo Spinelli's photographs in 1996 while searching for illustrations for a book on World War II American and German POWs.[2] I wanted something dramatic and unusual, so I selected an unforgettable Spinelli photo of an American prisoner bribing his German guard (see p. 3). Spinelli generously granted permission to use this photo, and I thought this was the end of our contact. Some three years later, however, Spinelli called me. He had just donated his entire collection to the POW Museum at the Andersonville National Historic Site in Andersonville, Georgia, and he wondered if I might be interested in helping him do a book centered on his highly unusual photographs. By this time, a number of his photographs had found their way into print, but such a book would allow his unforgettable shots of life behind barbed wire to receive the kind of national exposure we both felt they deserved.

✪

WORLD WAR II holds a special fascination for Americans who continue to praise the contributions and sacrifices of the men who fought in the so-called Good War. Few would argue with NBC news anchor and author Tom Brokaw who lauded these men as America's "Greatest Generation." However, the 95,000 Americans who had the misfortune to become prisoners of war have not shared equally in this universal praise.[3]

Trading with the enemy.

In the popular mind it was no honor to become a POW—unless, of course, you escaped. Unfortunately, successful escapes occurred primarily in novels and movies. For example, in Stalag IIIB, where Angelo Spinelli was interned, out of 150 attempted escapes only one was successful.[4] The overwhelming majority of prisoners lacked either the opportunity or the will to escape. Instead, most sat out their captivity, suffering in silence and often with a sense of defeat and shame, especially when they thought back on their fallen buddies left behind on the fields of battle.

Many popular notions and misconceptions contributed to the prisoners' immediate and long-term sense of failure and guilt. After all, John Wayne was never captured! Sylvester Stallone was, but only to escape and exact his bloody revenge as the indestructible Rambo. An anonymous general insisted that becoming a prisoner of war represented "a failed mission," and failure is something Americans seldom willingly accept. Imagine the effect of receiving a letter from a loving wife that concluded, "Even though you are a coward and a failure, I still love you." Similarly, a thank you note from a prisoner to an unknown woman who had knitted him a sweater elicited this reply: "I'm sorry you got it. I wish it had gone to someone on active duty." One misguided father naively wrote his POW son, "I hope you are able to get in plenty of golf, and don't drink too much of that good German beer; it is very fattening." Such stories were common, and although some were certainly apocryphal, the prisoners nevertheless heard them, often after returning home, where they heightened their sense of shame.

Angelo Spinelli was typical of most returning prisoners. After briefly being honored at the 1945 YMCA luncheon and by the publication the following year of *The Yankee Kriegies*, Spinelli spent years suffering in silence, in spite of the fact that he was certainly one of the genuine heroes of the Second World War. We can only hope that his story and photographs provide a healthy antidote to popular misconceptions of life as a prisoner and to any feelings of shame former POWs might continue to harbor.

✿

OF THE MORE THAN 1,000 photographs Spinelli risked his life to take, some 400 are of excellent quality. They feature prisoners trading with the guards, combating ticks, lice, and other vermin, preparing meager rations on ingenious cooking contraptions, fighting off boredom by playing baseball, soccer, and basketball, putting on musical and dramatic presentations, and worshiping in a chapel the prisoners themselves had built. There is also an unforgettable shot of the lifeless body of a Russian prisoner who was shot reaching for a cigarette an American had thrown over the compound fence *(see photo, p. 6)*.

A few years ago, one of Spinelli's photographs produced an unexpected but very positive result. When former prisoner Charles Dreier died on January 19, 1985, his widow, Agatha Dreier, who was entitled to military benefits, could not prove her late husband had been a POW. A fire in St. Louis had destroyed his military records, and she had no idea how to proceed. Fortunately, one of Angelo Spinelli's photographs proved her case. Unmistakably, there was Charles Dreier playing the piano for Stalag IIIB's prisoner orchestra, called "The Yankee Doodlers" *(see photo, p. 8)*.

Clydie Morgan, who at the time was the national adjutant of the

Angelo Spinelli risked his life to document the crumbled body of this Russian prisoner *(see arrow)*, who was shot and killed for reaching under the warning fence trying to retrieve a cigarette an American had thrown him. More than 3,000,000 Russian POWs died in German prison camps. Joseph Stalin's refusal to sign the 1929 Geneva Accord meant Russian prisoners had no access to Red Cross parcels or international guarantees of humane treatment. Even more devastating was the contempt with which the leaders of the Third Reich held all Russians. Propaganda Minister Joseph Goebbels called them "a conglomeration of animals"; Hitler referred to them simply as "the Mongol Half-Wits."

American Ex-Prisoners of War Association, reveals that Spinelli's photos "have been used in therapy and to jog memories the men didn't know they had."[5] True enough, but they also allow the rest of us, albeit vicariously, to experience life in a German prison camp.

Angelo Spinelli also kept a secret notebook in which he recorded books he received and read, contents of packages from home, including an accounting of the precious cigarettes and cigars he used for bartering, and sundry personal items he requested and received from the International Red Cross, the YMCA, and the Service Men's Relief of Baltimore *(see Appendix, pp. 196–201).*

✪

STALAG IIIB, where Spinelli took most of his photographs, was located three-quarters of a mile northwest of the small town of Fürstenberg on the east bank of the Oder Spree Canal, some sixty miles southeast of Berlin.[6] A few miles farther to the east was the Oder River, which, along with the Neisse River, forms the eastern boundary of present-day Germany.

The camp was approximately 870 yards by 870 yards and surrounded by a triple barbed wire fence, with several menacing guard towers looming overhead *(see p. 40).* Among its approximately 25,000 prisoners were Russians, French, Serbians, Croatians, and, by January 31, 1945, when the camp was evacuated, almost 5,000 Americans, most of whom were U.S. Army noncommissioned officers.

The first American prisoners arrived in Stalag IIIB early in 1943. Like Spinelli, who arrived on March 29, 1943, most had been captured in North Africa. The majority of the later arrivals were taken prisoner

The Yankee Doodlers, bringing in the New Year of 1944. These were highly skilled musicians who had been members of a regimental band when they were captured and sent to Stalag IIIB. The YMCA donated the instruments and the International Red Cross delivered them to the prison camp. The musicians had to remain still for this ten-second time exposure. Among those who played with the Yankee Doodlers (not all in this photo) were Lou Boettcher, Nebraska, alto sax and band leader; Al Gasper, California, trombone; Harley Collins, Iowa, trombone; Bob Purdue, Iowa, trombone; Gus Hahn, Iowa, trumpet; Don Whittaker, Iowa, trumpet; Dale Arnold, Iowa, trumpet; Russ "Doc" Dougherty, New Jersey, tenor sax; Dale Thompson, Iowa, tenor sax; Ray Deford, Indiana, alto sax; Dick Gray, California, baritone sax; Ed Henry, West Virginia, accordion; Charlie Dreier, New York, piano; Johnny Triano, New York, guitar; Joe Reeder, New Jersey, drums; Dave Mandich, Pennsylvania, bass; Henry Smith, New Jersey, vocalist; Russ Christian, Texas, trombone; George Miller, piano; Frank Benventano, violin and accordion; Edward Smith, base and tuba. A half century later, the widow of Charlie Dreier (on piano above) used this Angelo Spinelli photo to prove to the government that her husband had indeed been a prisoner.

after the June 6, 1944, Normandy invasion, and especially after the Battle of the Bulge, which began on December 16, 1944.

The American compound, which measured 100 by 670 yards, initially consisted of six wooden barracks, each housing some 300 men. By early 1945, the American compound had expanded to twelve barracks, with up to 450 men in each of the buildings. Behind the barracks was a spacious field where the prisoners could stroll, play games, or prepare individual meals. In the middle of this field was a small building for the American Man of Confidence (MOC) and his assistant, who represented the interests of the American prisoners before the German camp administrators. M.Sgt. Clyde M. Bennett, S.Sgt. Arthur S. Taylor, and S.Sgt. Joseph C. Gasperich served as MOC during Spinelli's twenty-two months in Stalag IIIB.

The barracks were divided into two sections, separated from each other by lavatories containing cold-water spigots and by a small room that individuals could use as a kitchen. Triple-decker beds were arranged on one side of the barracks with tables and benches on the other side. At each end of the building was a primitive urinal that was used only at night. The barracks were heated by large brick stoves, but the quantity and quality of the coal was inadequate, even for mild winter days. An additional barracks, furnished and decorated primarily with items sent by the YMCA and the International Red Cross, included a recreation hall, theater, classroom, chapel, and a library containing 10,800 volumes.

According to author Tim Wolter, who incorporated many of Angelo Spinelli's photographs in his book on POW baseball, Stalag IIIB "was a curious mixture of harshness and leniency. The guards were constantly harassing the prisoners in small ways: withholding Red Cross parcels for minor infractions, insisting on puncturing all canned goods to prevent hoarding for escapes, and tossing offenders into the cooler with liberality. But in other ways the prisoners got away with a lot. There was an active trade in all commodities across the fences with the Russians and the French, and the Americans were given little or no punishment when caught. Of course, several Russians were shot on the spot for their end of the transaction."[7]

The German *Kommandant* of Stalag IIIB was *Oberst* (Colonel) Blau. *Oberleutnant* (First Lieutenant) Gross served as *Lager* (Camp) Officer and *Feldwebel* (Sergeant) Schoen as *Lager* NCO. Blau, who was seldom seen by the prisoners and who reportedly committed suicide just days before the end of the war, appears to have been an able and fair administrator who adhered closely to the principles of the 1929 Geneva Accord.[8] Gross and Schoen seemingly delighted in harassing the prisoners and were very much disliked. Gross typically held long roll calls *(Appell)*, often in the coldest weather. He also conducted frequent searches, and confiscated the prisoners' food and cigarettes for the flimsiest of reasons.

The most fascinating of the German officers was *Leutnant* (Lieutenant) F. W. Von Fricken, who as camp administrative officer served as the liaison between Colonel Blau and the American Man of Confidence. Von Fricken had lived in Yonkers, New York, in the 1920s, spoke excellent English, and was so friendly with the Americans that they were undecided whether he was a German or an American spy. Angelo Spinelli often chatted with him and even offered him cigarettes for the camera he so desperately wanted to acquire. Von Fricken turned

The German officer on the left is Lt. F. W. Von Fricken, with whom Angelo Spinelli established a friendship that extended even beyond the war. This is the only photo in the Spinelli collection not taken with one of his two cameras. Spinelli does not know who actually took it but does remember bartering for it with another GI.

him down; nevertheless, Spinelli remembers swapping cigarettes with him for fresh eggs, and Von Fricken recalls that Spinelli "had no equal when it came to bartering."[9] After the war, they renewed their friendship at a 1986 meeting in New Jersey, at which Von Fricken gave Spinelli the only surviving copy of the camp newspaper, the *POW-WOW (see Appendix, p. 182)*, and a copy of his article, "The Memorable Memorial Day of 1943," which he was hoping to publish. Interestingly, Von Fricken was able to return to the United States after the war, in part because Dr. Roland Marti, a top official with the International Red Cross, had granted him a certificate that stated, "The American prisoners of war owe their relatively good physical and spiritual state in large part to F. W. Von Fricken who did everything in his power to facilitate their survival."[10] Von Fricken became an American citizen in 1963 and remained in contact with Spinelli until he died in 1999 at the age of ninety-four.

On balance, Stalag IIIB was not a badly run camp. Certainly, conditions were better than in many of the other camps, and especially in those holding enlisted men, where the prisoners seldom had the kind of recreational, religious, and library facilities available in IIIB.[11] Enlisted men also were less likely to receive Red Cross packages, and in some of the work camps they never received these badly needed food parcels.[12] There were also other reasons why the men in IIIB did better than their counterparts in other camps. Their proximity to Berlin meant their mail and Red Cross parcels arrived with a degree of regularity, and they could expect more frequent inspections by the International Red Cross, as mandated in the Geneva Accord.[13] The International Red Cross was also responsible for packages and other amenities arriving from the United States, and these too were distributed from Berlin.

A little known but fascinating incident occurred in Stalag IIIB early in November 1944. The guards ordered the prisoners in the American compound to turn in all spare field jackets, overcoats, and trousers, allegedly for the use of new prisoners who had insufficient clothing. In reality, the German *Wehrmacht* was planning to dress some units in American uniforms for its surprise counterattack in the Ardennes on

December 16, 1944. This became, of course, the Battle of the Bulge, Germany's last major offensive of World War II. Some of the prisoners in IIIB did turn in their extra clothing, but others, such as S.Sgt. Jack T. Sneesby, "smelled a rat and word was passed to render everything not being worn unserviceable."[14]

Without question, the YMCA helped make life more tolerable in Stalag IIIB, as well as in many other camps. On June 21, 1945, a group of high ranking Air Corps officers, who had themselves been prisoners in Germany, sent a memo to their commanding general in Washington commending the YMCA for its great service to American POWs: "It was largely through the efforts of the YMCA that the mental attitude of the prisoners of war remained so fine throughout their incarceration in Germany," wrote the officers. "We cannot commend and praise the YMCA too much for the magnificent work they performed for the prisoners of war, and we hold that it was largely through their efforts that the officers of the AAF prisoners of war returned to the United States in such fine mental and physical condition."[15]

The YMCA, acting through the International Red Cross, furnished the prisoners Bibles, hymn books, tracts, and other items needed to conduct religious services. It also sent a wide array of recreational equipment, including baseball and basketball uniforms. In addition, it sent scripts for plays, and such related sundries as electrical fixtures, costumes, makeup, wigs, and sufficient musical instruments to form an orchestra. Also included were novels and reference books, as well as textbooks, paper, pencils, protractors, chalk, and blackboards that were used in the many courses offered in some of the camps, including

IIIB.[16] Representatives from the YMCA regularly visited the camps, often bringing with them messages from loved ones and taking back similar missives. Unfortunately, not all the camps received materials from the YMCA, and again, the enlisted men's camps were the least likely to receive them or, if they did, little opportunity to use them because their frequent work details, both inside and outside the camps, left them with neither the time nor the energy to do much but eat and sleep.[17]

Keeping busy was the best antidote for the boredom, inertia, and depression, sometimes referred to as "barbed-wire psychosis," that all too often afflicted prisoners. S.Sergeant Jack Sneesby well understood the importance of keeping active to retain one's mental and physical health:

> Two personality groups began to appear: Those who were up and active all or part of the day to stay warm, and those who crawled back under their blanket and shivered all day to stay warm. . . . The active group spent time reading, playing single or double solitaire, walking around the compound, and BS'ing. The latter died out after hearing everyone's "story" and favorite recipes over and over again. We also could participate in or enjoy the camp orchestra, chorus, chapel, theater, library, classes, and outdoor sports. A windup phonograph and some well worn classical records rotated among the barracks for an evening of entertainment.
>
> Three activities took up a fair part of each day. We were rousted out each morning and afternoon for *Appell* [roll call]. The guards tramped through the barracks making sure everyone was out. The *Appell* could take from a half hour for a simple count to a day, de-

pending on our cooperation and whether the Jerries wanted to search the barracks for contraband. The Americans were most ingenious in their hassling of the Germans during the count and by their undisciplined behavior *(see photos, pp. 16 and 17).*

The other two activities had to do with eating: warm acorn coffee in the morning after *Appell,* which was good for shaving, and later in the day soup, potatoes, bread, and, if we were fortunate, our portion of a Red Cross parcel.

Each evening we looked forward to the nightly news from the BBC. With a sentry placed at the door to warn of approaching strangers, someone came through the barracks and read the daily news which was great for our morale.[18] This same system kept us informed of camp activities.[19]

Despite the fact that Stalag IIIB was arguably the best-run NCO camp, and certainly much better than those holding enlisted men, life for POWs was never easy. Food, clothing, and warmth were always lacking. Even more destructive to a prisoner's well-being was the mental anguish. Except for several photos of men looking pensively at the barbed wire, psychological distress was all but impossible for Angelo Spinelli to capture on film. At times, all prisoners felt alone and forgotten. Facing an uncertain future, they were constantly tormented by feelings of apprehension and anxiety.[20] Exacerbating such fears were rumors such as the one that suggested POWs would be court-martialed after the war for having allowed themselves to be captured.[21] The greatest fear, however, as Angelo Spinelli makes clear in his narrative, was that they would never return home alive, especially after Heinrich Himmler's *SS* reportedly took over the administration of the

Early morning *Appell* (roll call) in Stalag IIIB. The men stood in columns of fives waiting for the German guards to make their count. If the count was incorrect, the guards would start over. Notice the man at the lower right (above) sneaking behind the last column to be counted again. He is either covering for someone missing, such as Angelo Spinelli who took this photograph from the latrine, or for someone who was attempting an escape.

In this shot of the morning *Appell*, a prisoner is squatting down just to confuse the count. Of course, in cold weather the men wanted the *Appell* to finish as quickly as possible.

POW camps in the fall of 1944. Rumors circulated among the prisoners that Hitler intended to hold them as hostages to get better peace terms,[22] or, even more disturbing, that he had ordered *SS Death Squads* to execute all prisoners rather than allow them to be liberated.[23]

✪

BECAUSE THE Russian armies were closing in from the east, the Germans evacuated Stalag IIIB on January 31, 1945, and Angelo Spinelli and his fellow prisoners were forced to march some sixty-five miles to the west to Stalag IIIA at Luckenwalde. Such forced marches were common in the closing months of the war, and because of the bitter cold, insufficient clothing, and weakened condition of the prisoners, they could be deadly.[24] In fact, Spinelli himself became incapacitated and would have lost his life but for the help of two courageous fellow prisoners.

The departure from Stalag IIIB was so hasty that the prisoners were provided with no provisions and had little or nothing to eat until the third day when each received a small piece of bread. For the remainder of their seven-day march each man received a loaf of bread and one-eighth of a tin of cheese. Water was also in short supply, as William Kalway so vividly recalls:

> I don't know how many thousands of prisoners there were, but it seemed as though the whole countryside was one moving mass of men. After a few hours, most of us were so tired that we got rid of everything but our blanket and mess kit. . . . The Germans fed us absolutely nothing for the first two days, and the only water we had was from scooping up snow. . . . One time we heard an SS officer telling

the officer in charge of our section that if we didn't move fast enough, he should order the guards to shoot us. Several times we had to step over the bodies of Americans who had been shot. At least one of our men who had stopped to urinate was also shot.[25]

Jack T. Sneesby also remembers the horrors of the march from Stalag IIIB to IIIA:

Then came the order to march. German soldiers moving slowly eastward, over snow-clogged, ice-glazed roads; five thousand American soldiers, four abreast, plodded slowly westward in the sub-zero darkness.

Slipping, falling, bumping, cursing, the line crawled slowly toward safety. Soon the road was littered with broken sleds, pack sacks, bundles, extra coats, "blowers" [cookers], anything to lighten the load. But the line kept moving all night and all the next day. Finally a night's "rest" in an old barn.

Scenes from the march still are vivid in my memory. Mounted German soldiers riding their horses down the snow-covered ridge to force exhausted GIs to their feet and back on the road. A night time foray from a guarded barn to steal potatoes out of straw-covered piles in a nearby field. The German farm wife who handed out slices of black bread till the loaf was exhausted. Elderly *Volksturm* guards moaning as they marched. The still form of a GI, lying in his own blood, shot for some unknown reason by a guard, covered by his short French overcoat, his Polish cap with the "crazy" eagle lying trampled in the mud.[26]

George Rosie was another American who witnessed the killing of prisoners on this deadly march:

One POW walked over to an old German woman standing by her fence and tried to trade a bar of soap for some food. One of the guards walked up behind him and smacked him in the back of the head with his rifle. He dropped like a sack of potatoes. As we were marched into the barn, we walked by him, but there was no sign of life. The back of his head was smashed in and he was bleeding profusely. . . . Later that day we took another break, and as the guards were getting us back on the road we heard a shot. Apparently at the head of the column one of the Airborne guys didn't get up quickly enough to suit one of the guards, so he shot him right in the forehead. As we walked by, he was lying on his back by the side of the road.[27]

✪

WHEN A VERY SICK and exhausted Spinelli and his fellow Americans arrived at Stalag IIIA in Luckenwalde on February 7, 1945, they soon discovered that conditions were far worse than in IIIB. Stalag IIIA contained approximately 38,000 prisoners, including almost 6,000 Americans, many of whom had just arrived from other camps. The constant and deadly bombing raids and fast closing Allied forces often prevented the Red Cross parcels from reaching the prisoners, and the Germans did not have enough food for their own troops, let alone for their POWs. The prisoners were thus reduced to as little as a single slice of bread a day, and, if lucky, some watery soup. Stalag IIIA was so badly overcrowded that most of the men from Stalag IIIB had to bivouac outside the camp itself. The fortunate ones were crammed into tents, but others had no shelter at all. According to William Kalway, the appalling conditions had a dreadful effect on the men:

Luckenwalde was by far the worst camp I had been in. I later read about Andersonville, the Civil War Confederate prison, but I believe Stalag IIIA was equally bad. We lived under unspeakable conditions. A lot of the men were assigned to open areas with no protection. We were so crowded that it was absolutely impossible to maintain even the rudimentary conditions of cleanliness. . . . The mental condition of the men began to deteriorate rapidly. This deterioration took many forms. Mostly, the men would just sit and stare into space. If you asked a question, you received a blank stare for about a minute before the person realized you had asked him something. Then his answer was so disjointed, you wondered if he really understood the question. Some men refused to speak at all, and several times individuals had to be forcefully restrained from rushing the fence to commit suicide.[28]

Because he had become deathly ill on the forced march and because of the brutal conditions in IIIA, Angelo Spinelli took few photographs during his final months as a prisoner of war. All this changed, however, after the Russians liberated Luckenwalde on April 22, 1945. Spinelli was then able to take photographs of Russian tanks and soldiers moving through IIIA, Americans celebrating their release, the arrival of American Red Cross ambulances to transport the sick and wounded, and a captured German truck on which Spinelli rode to freedom. Spinelli had also found another camera in a downed German fighter plane that he used to take many of these post-liberation shots.

Spinelli's final photographs are of Camp Lucky Strike in northern France, where the assembled American soldiers awaited transportation home, their sea voyage on a Liberty ship, and, finally, their triumphant arrival in New York Harbor on June 13, 1945. Toting his musette bag, containing two cameras and his precious negatives, some of which went all the way back to his combat service in North Africa twenty-six long months before, Angelo Spinelli was home!

✪

ON APRIL 9, 2000, fifty-five years after his liberation, Angelo Spinelli donated his incomparable collection of photographs to the National Park Service's National Prisoner of War Museum at Andersonville, Georgia. Park Ranger Fred Sanchez promised Spinelli that his negatives would be safely preserved, although prints made from them would be readily available for future generations. That same year, Andersonville's Eric Reinert, Alan Marsh, and Sanchez put together a traveling exhibit of the Spinelli photographs titled "Behind the Barbed Wire: Angelo Spinelli's Photo-Documentation on Life and Culture in a POW Stalag Camp," which circulated through various military and civilian museums and public libraries. In 2003, the exhibit found a permanent home in the Italian American Museum in New York City.

✪

IT IS IMPOSSIBLE to put a historical or monetary value on Angelo Spinelli's photographs. They are, in fact, priceless. Although a few other photos of POWs do exist, nothing portrays the daily life of American prisoners in Nazi Germany as does his collection. In a recent article in the *Atlanta Journal Constitution*, Fred Sanchez acknowledges that every time Spinelli took one of his 1,000 pictures, "He was performing way beyond the call of duty."[29] Eric Reinert, a former curator at the Andersonville National Historic Site, agrees: "There is no other single collection of artifacts that documents life as a POW of the Germans like this one," writes Reinert. "It will become even more important once those who experienced captivity are gone."[30] But no one has summed up the importance of Spinelli's photographs better than Joe DiMare, a fellow POW from Stalag IIIB: "Today, each picture in Spinelli's spectacular collection of photos tells an exciting story, a vivid portrayal of drama, pathos, tragedy, and, yes, even humor," writes DiMare. "Fame is fickle and fleeting [but] Spinelli's photos will always be alive in the eyes of history!"[31]

The case can certainly be made that for his heroism and valor while a prisoner of war, Angelo Spinelli deserves the highest military honors and arguably even the Medal of Honor. In 1989, U.S. Senator Connie Mack of Florida inquired of the Department of Defense if Angelo Spinelli was not indeed deserving of such recognition. Lt. Col. Leland W. Klein, the U.S. Army's Congressional Coordinator, replied that although Spinelli's photographs were "a noteworthy achievement," they did not warrant such consideration because "in the absence of a written recommendation for an award submitted prior to May 1951, there is no authority whereby he may now be awarded a military decoration after so many years have passed."[32] In response, Spinelli pointed out that his photos themselves should have served as the highest "authority," and they had certainly been taken before the May 1951 deadline. But even if his photographs never receive the kind of official recognition they so richly deserve, Angelo Spinelli remains profoundly grateful that they have now been safely preserved for future generations.

Sgt. Angelo Spinelli

ANGELO SPINELLI'S NARRATIVE

Angelo Spinelli first told his story shortly after being repatriated at a YMCA ceremony honoring a group of former POWs. After seeing Spinelli's photographs, the YMCA staff published a small booklet in 1946 titled *Yankee Kriegies: How Our POWs Made "Little Americas" Behind Nazi Barbed Wire*. Spinelli's secret photographs did not surface again publicly until several appeared in the 1981 Time-Life book, *Prisoners of World War II*. Over the past few years, Spinelli and his photographs have enjoyed increasing exposure through numerous newspaper and magazine articles, television documentaries and news features, and national exhibitions. The first-person narrative that follows has been culled from all these sources, as well as from several personal interviews.

AFTER I WAS CAPTURED, there wasn't a day that went by that I didn't think I might die. Some of the guards and camp officers used to tell us we'd never get out alive, but at that age I really didn't have any fear. I figured if I was going to die, at least I would try to leave behind some evidence of how we lived as prisoners. I hoped someone would eventually see my photographs, but it was all a gamble.

Nobody believed I could have taken these pictures—until they saw them. I marvel myself that I was able to do so. I took them knowing that I always had someone watching me. I just had faith in the Blessed Mother that I would not get caught. When I went overseas, my future wife gave me a picture of the Blessed Mother and a printed prayer. I kept them with me at all times, and each of them did so much to keep me alive. In fact, I still have them.

✪

I WAS BORN March 14, 1917, in the Bronx, the second child of Domenica and Giacomo Spinelli. My parents had both emigrated from a small town in southern Italy called Casamassima, which was near the larger city of Bari. I grew up in St. Lucy's Parish in the Bronx where I was an altar boy and absorbed the faith that would help me survive the prison camps.

I fell in love with photography while I was attending Evander Childs High School where I was the photographer for the school paper. I had managed to buy a used German 35mm Contax camera and a Kodak camera as well. This friend of mine, Herbert Carlin, who later became a dean of engineering at Cornell University, and I built a dark room in his house, so we could process our own film.

Our family suffered a terrible tragedy shortly before I graduated high school. My father was killed in an accident while working for the Department of Sanitation in New York. In spite of my father's death, I wanted to continue my studies so I tried to work my way through college. That was during the depression, and I was lucky to get any kind of work. I finally got a job learning the jewelry trade. In the evening, I took classes at City College of New York. This went on for seven years; then, I got drafted and they wouldn't let me finish. I went into the army on July 25, 1941.

Signal Corps cameraman Angelo Spinelli at Camp Joseph T. Robinson in Little Rock, Arkansas, shortly before being shipped overseas.

NORTH AFRICA

AFTER BASIC TRAINING, I was assigned to the Signal Corps as a public relations and combat photographer and sent overseas. On October 26, 1942, after a brief stay in Great Britain, we shipped out from Glasgow, Scotland, on the New Zealand ship *H.M.S. Awatea*, as part of Operation Torch, which was the enormous Allied amphibious invasion of North Africa. All the soldiers had to stay below deck, but we cameramen insisted we had to be topside in case there might be enemy planes or submarines that we could photograph.

Fellow Signal Corps soldier Samuel Steinberg took this November 1942 photo of Angelo Spinelli filming their convoy from the rail of the *H.M.S. Awatea* heading for the North African campaign. When Spinelli was captured, the Germans took his gun, camera, and unexposed film, but allowed him to keep a roll of exposed film when he explained it only had personal pictures on it. The photographs on the following seven pages are from this roll of film, which Spinelli kept hidden during his twenty-six months of captivity.

Spinelli (left) and two other Signal Corp soldiers work on their camera equipment on board
the *H.M.S. Awatea*, which left Glasgow, Scotland, on October 26, 1942, and arrived in
Algiers on November 8 for the Battle of North Africa.

Angelo Spinelli at rest on board the *H.M.S. Awatea*!

AFTER WE LANDED at Algiers on November 8, 1942, I was assigned to the First Armored Division where at first I mostly photographed awards, speeches, and ceremonies, but then I also began taking pictures behind enemy lines. My combat and behind-the-lines reconnaissance photography earned me the Legion of Merit from General Eisenhower's Headquarters. The date on the award was November 19, 1943. Of course, I had to receive this honor in absentia, because by that time I had already spent nine months as a prisoner of war in Nazi Germany. It was only after my liberation and my return to the States, that I had the chance to read what my Legion of Merit said about my work:

> For exceptionally meritorious conduct in the performance of outstanding services from 8 November 1942 to approximately 18 February 1943. Sgt. Spinelli . . . penetrated enemy territory for days at a time in obtaining reconnaissance photographs of enemy terrain and installations. After successful completion of this mission which involved advancing with combat forces to Algiers and Bone, he voluntarily accepted a hazardous assignment to photograph medical procedures in the front lines for a combat medical history. Sgt. Spinelli, by superior knowledge of his profession, coolness in the face of enemy fire, and devotion to duty, played an important part in making records of great historical significance.
>
> By command of General Eisenhower,
> E. L. Ford,
> Brigadier General, SC, Chief of Staff

Before I was captured I received another form of recognition. Col. Darryl Zanuck, the famous Hollywood movie producer and owner, visited my Signal Corps unit in Algiers. He was collecting battlefield photographs and film, and he thought we were doing such a good job, that he gave me and a couple of my buddies a bottle of French cognac.

Hollywood movie mogul Col. Darryl F. Zanuck (left) presenting Spinelli (second from right) and his two buddies with their well-deserved bottle of cognac.

Combat photographer Angelo Spinelli took this picture his second day in North Africa.

Angelo Spinelli spent more than three months in North Africa working as a combat photographer before he was captured on Valentine's Day, February 14, 1943.

CAPTURED!

I HAD BEEN IN North Africa for just over three months when I was captured. I was on a combat photographic mission near the Fiad Pass in Tunisia when my film and luck ran out at the same time. I was sitting around without much to do when this lieutenant ordered me and three others to move some fifteen German prisoners to the rear. We loaded them on a truck and started off. We hadn't gone very far before we drove smack into the middle of a tank battle. There weren't supposed to be any tanks around, but there certainly were, and they were giving our guys a devil of a pasting. There wasn't time to do anything but stop the truck and dive behind a mound of dirt. All of us, American guards and German prisoners, huddled together, forgetting that we were enemies in the common hope that we would not be killed. After a while, the shooting stopped, and when we looked up, a German tank was pointing its guns down at us. The American tanks were all shot up and on fire. Michael Alfonsi, who was our driver, panicked and wanted to use his .45 pistol against the tank. I stopped him, and I figure that saved our lives. Right then and there, we changed places with our prisoners, and we became Yankee *Kriegies*.[1] The date was February 14, 1943 — Valentine's Day.

✪

AFTER WE WERE CAPTURED, our German prisoners told an officer that we had treated them well. We had fed them, given them cigarettes, and returned their personal belongings. I was even able to communicate a little with them with my high school French. My philosophy

North African terrain.

was to have empathy for even your worst enemy. Be good to everyone because you never know when you may need them. I'm sure I'm alive today because we had handled our German prisoners with compassion.

For the next few days we were treated very respectfully. I was allowed to keep my musette bag with all my personal items, including some undeveloped film I had taken in North Africa. They took us by truck to the Sebastian Villa, which was a German interrogation center on the Mediterranean Sea. On the way we picked up an American lieutenant who was so frightened he took off his insignia and told us to call him by his first name. We had heard stories of Germans killing Allied prisoners and of our forces killing some of the soldiers they captured. But we were locked up in a nice room, and our German guards provided us with excellent meals. One of the officers even gave us cigars. We were questioned, but nothing more than name, rank, and serial number. The interrogating officers didn't try any rough stuff, but one of them warned us that the farther we got from the fighting, and the closer we got to Germany, the worse we would fare. He wasn't wrong!

Before we left, the Germans took us to a radio station where we made a statement that we were well and that the Red Cross should be contacted and told where we were. This broadcast was picked up in the States by someone at the New York *Daily News*, which then published a feature article about it, including a photo of my driver, Michael Alfonsi.[2] My family and my fiancée's family heard about it so they knew I was alive and was being sent to Germany.

The Germans then put us on a JU-52 plane that flew us to Capua, Italy, which was near Naples. After we landed, this Italian officer asked if any of us were Italians, but no one said anything. Then he said to us in Italian, "You who are Italians are traitors to the fatherland." They had the guns so I wasn't about to argue with them. I just pretended I didn't know Italian. All this left us in a kind of daze. I really expected to be killed, and I was thinking what my last meal would be like.

We stayed there about a week or ten days, and then they took us to the train station and jammed us like animals into these 40-and-8 boxcars, so called because they could carry forty men or eight horses. They locked us in with no water or food, and we started off to Munich. The bucket we were supposed to use for a toilet soon overflowed, and the whole car reeked of urine and feces. It was hours before they opened the door and gave us something to eat. We really didn't know if we were going to make it or not. We were in shock and very depressed. The saving thing was that we were young and in reasonably good health.

We finally arrived at Stalag 7A at Moosburg just northeast of Munich. We stayed there for only a few days before being reloaded on the same kind of boxcars and shipped to Stalag IIIB where I would spend my next twenty-two months.

Stalag IIIB.

STALAG IIIB–FÜRSTENBERG/ODER

We arrived in Stalag IIIB on March 29, 1943. On that first day, one of the guards told us we would never get out alive, and those words stayed with me every moment I was a prisoner.

I later learned from Lt. F. W. Von Fricken, who was one of the German officers in Stalag IIIB, and whom I would meet again in New Jersey after the war, that the camp contained some 3,500 Americans, 12,000 Russians, 8,000 Frenchmen, and 1,000 Serbians. Stalag IIIB was for noncommissioned officers, with the enlisted men and officers sent to other camps.

There were guard towers manned by soldiers with machine guns and search lights. They commanded the alleys formed by the barbed wire, and it was sure death to get caught in that "no-man's land." We were the first Americans in Stalag IIIB and were put in our own compound. There was a double row of barbed wire that separated our compound from those containing other nationalities. There was also a ten-foot warning wire, and if you crossed this wire into the so-called "warning zone," the guards would shoot you.

The first thing they did was give us a tetanus shot right in the chest. It was very cold, and at first we had no heat so we had to sleep with all our clothes on. We slept on straw mattresses that were filled with mice, fleas, ticks, and lice. I slept with a blanket over my head, but I could still feel them crawling over me. One night we caught twenty-three mice. We would turn one of our benches upside down, and then use little slivers of wood about the size of a toothpick to prop it up. We would put a little piece of cheese on these pieces of wood, and when the mice would nibble on it, the bench would collapse on them.

Some of our guys ripped out the window frames and burned them for heat. We never thought we would be there that long. The Germans did not replace them so we just had to live with the cold. We had one stove in our barracks, and after a period of time some of the guys volunteered to go out on wood details, which also allowed them to steal potatoes and other kinds of food. However, once I had my camera, I didn't dare go with them. I had to stay near my equipment in case there was a shakedown.

We did have a washroom in our building, but it had just a few cold-water spigots for more than 300 men. If we wanted hot water, we had to haul it from the kitchen, if there was some available.

We had one large latrine toward the rear of the camp. When it was full, the Russian prisoners came and shoveled it out into a "honey wagon," which was then spread on nearby farmers' fields.

Opposite: This ominous sign, which was clearly a literal translation from the German, was posted between the American and Russian compounds in Stalag IIIB. Two fences separated the various compounds, with approximately a three-foot no-man's zone between them. Several prisoners were shot for violating this space, and a nervous guard once took a shot at Spinelli for trying to retrieve a baseball that had rolled under the fence.

Wash Day! Initially, the American prisoners were housed in six such barracks in Stalag IIIB, each holding approximately 300 prisoners. Later another six barracks were added and as many as 450 men were crammed into a single barracks. The barracks were divided into A and B sections. Angelo Spinelli, for example, lived in Barracks 19B.

Prisoners had to wait patiently in line for buckets of hot water to use for bathing and washing clothes. There was never enough of this precious commodity. The two men in the foreground are carrying a half barrel of ersatz coffee. Spinelli took this shot looking out through the door of his barracks.

Back of the American compound on a cold, winter day. The serpentine, in-ground air raid
shelter on the left was built at the insistence of the International Red Cross. It was while
standing in this trench that Angelo Spinelli took his unforgettable shot of the guard tower *(see
photo, p. 40)*. The building on the right housed the American Man of Confidence (MOC),
who represented the prisoners' interests with the German camp officials. S.Sgt. Joseph C.
Gasperich was serving as MOC at the time of this photo. Notice the two prisoners taking their
daily walk around the American compound.

The American compound in Stalag IIIB. At the lower left is the Seal of the United States, built from colored glass, which the prisoners had traded for in nearby Fürstenberg where there were several glass factories. A German camp officer named Gross asked what the mosaic meant. When told it represented the United States, he destroyed the seal with his boot. Spinelli remembered, "I cried when I saw that happen. It was like freedom destroyed."

THE GUARDS in our camp were either very old, very young, or recovering from wounds. Some of the older ones who had been wounded in battle or who had lost family members, no longer cared about much of anything. But the guards were nothing like those on *Hogan's Heroes*, which always portrayed them as stupid. Most were anything but. If you tried to get by with too much, you got into trouble, but as long as you regarded them as human beings, you were all right. However, none of us ever tried to talk to the *SS*![3]

Initially, we called all guards "goons."[4] When they came into the compounds for inspections, guys would yell, "Goon up!" We called some of them "ferrets" because they were always snooping around. A ferret's assistant was a "weasel." Some of the guards told us they weren't Nazis and that their greatest fear was being sent to the Russian front. That was the punishment given them if something went wrong in the camp. So, they usually tipped us off when the *SS* was planning a visit. That gave us time to hide things that were *verboten*, such as radios, cameras, notebooks, weapons, and a flock of perfectly innocent objects that the *SS* might decide to dislike. In return, we tried not to make too much trouble for the guards, figuring that our lives were bad enough without making them any worse. We eventually learned that Germans were neither all good nor all bad. Our own POW newspaper urged us to use common sense:

POW-WOW Editorial
June 25, 1943 [5]

All right, let's look at the thing sensibly.

"Patriotism" of a small handful of troublemakers, to the extent of making the 2,000-odd men miserable, is one thing.

Patriotism that realizes we are a sizable American group, in adverse circumstances, quite reasonably seeking to find whatever comfort we can here, is another thing.

It is hardly treason to display decency and sound common sense in our relations with our keepers. Far from being a betray [sic] of our own cause, it seems rather more to the point that our own country does actually command that we conduct ourselves as soldiers and gentlemen before foreign eyes.

The time is since gone when we could be of actual material service to America. If we wish to be of further service now, there is little more that we can do other than maintain the dignity and respect due her by acting as dignified and respectable emissaries in the hands of our captors.

Presently, this happens to be our "home." For how long, no one knows. We like to think our captivity will be brief, very brief, but who can say? Meanwhile, the foundation we lay of decent negotiations with our captors will be reflected in greater comfort, wider facilities, and more chance for self and group development in the near future and the future. This will determine what kind of men and citizens will eventually go home from these lagers.

Why make misery more miserable for the majority who are well-meaning and for those who are to come? Why impose the penalties of a false sense of patriotism as advocated by a selfish, indifferent minority upon the greater sense of patriotism recognized by the majority?

A soldier who makes a jackass out of himself before the eyes of our host does not represent the opinion and sentiment of this camp as a whole, but he does succeed in making our general burden a bit heavier to bear.

Our chances to be heroes were when we had the Garland in our grip. Let's not "put on the act" now—when it is too safely late.

You do not need to "sell out" our country to get along here. You do need, however, to act grown-up and think of the other fellow once in a while.

It is no pleasure being a P.O.W., but, so far as is consistent with loyalty and the restricted facilities at hand, we can make this camp a more pleasant abode. It is up to us.

And—it can be done.

Think it over.

✪

Life became better for Angelo Spinelli and his fellow prisoners after they were able to establish a daily routine and the Red Cross parcels began to arrive. In fact, German officer F. W. Von Fricken doubted "whether any GI could have survived his captivity without suffering severe and lasting damage to his health, if not worse, without the weekly comfort of the Red Cross parcels."[6] Angelo Spinelli remembers how hungry they all were before the Red Cross parcels began arriving on a regular basis in the summer of 1943.

BECAUSE WE COULDN'T be forced to work, we usually stayed in the sack until about 6:55 in the morning. Roll call was at 7:00, when we all had to pile out and line up in order to be counted by the German guards. We had to do this whether it was raining or snowing, and we had to stand there and get soaked or freeze until the Germans arrived at a figure that satisfied them. Three or four men would usually count us, and they had a hard time agreeing on the total. After that, we had breakfast, if there was something to eat.

The German ration for breakfast was usually only ersatz coffee. After breakfast we would be free to go to classes, play ball, or do anything we wanted. Lunch normally consisted of a watery soup. After lunch we were free again until late in the afternoon when there would be another roll call, and we'd all have to stand around outdoors and get counted again. For supper the Germans might give us a few potatoes, some ersatz bread, and maybe some meat.

We kept pretty good discipline against stealing one another's food. One fellow put aside his bread ration to eat later, and someone stole it. He got caught. The guys cut his hair into a T for Thief, and he had to go from barracks to barracks announcing, "I stole from my buddy. I stole from my buddy." After that there was very little stealing. You could leave your food on the table, and it would be there when you got back.

It was the Red Cross parcels that really saved us. They were supposed to arrive once a week and packages from home were permitted twice a month, but often they did not arrive. Without the Red Cross food parcels, it was pretty thin pickings. They contained chocolate, powdered milk, margarine, canned meat crackers, cigarettes, and various other things:[7]

The arrival of Red Cross parcels in the summer of 1943 undoubtedly helped forestall the ravages of severe malnutrition for Angelo Spinelli and his fellow prisoners in Stalag IIIB. Because of the camp's proximity to Berlin, these all-important packages arrived on a semi-regular schedule, at least until the fast-closing Russian troops forced the evacuation of IIIB on January 31, 1945.

S.Sgt. Joseph C. Gasperich, who as the American Man of Confidence represented the interests of the American prisoners with camp officials, discusses the arrival of Red Cross parcels with German officers.

Roland La Pointe from St. Louis and Silver Reed from Iowa waiting in bitterly cold weather for the arrival of Red Cross parcels that were long overdue.

55

Dividing up the contents of a Red Cross parcel.

Opposite: American POW Charles Wege shows off the first Christmas Red Cross Box to arrive in Stalag IIIB in 1943. The holiday packages always contained extra items for the men.

American POWs Nicholas D'Alessandro (left) and Hubert Wilhoff carry a half tub of soup for their barracks in Stalag IIIB. The soups were made from rutabagas, potatoes, or some kind of grain, with a few dead maggots floating on top.

An International Red Cross inspection found this kitchen in the American compound in Stalag IIIB to be spacious and well lit but lacking in utensils. The greater problem was having adequate food for this POW kitchen staff to cook.

Opposite: This building contained the main kitchen for the Americans in Stalag IIIB. The prisoners purchased some of the pots and pans hanging inside the window from the camp commissary, using camp money that they "earned," in compliance with the 1929 Geneva Accord.

Sitting around the "kitchen table" in their barracks in Stalag IIIB.
Michael J. Alfonsi (second from right) was driving the jeep when he
and Angelo Spinelli were captured in North Africa. Both were from
New York, and it was Alfonsi's voice on a German shortwave
broadcast the New York *Daily News* picked up on March 4, 1943:
"This is Michael J. Alfonsi," said the newly captured sergeant. "I
was taken prisoner in Tunisia and am going to Germany. Am in
good health. So long. Don't worry." Angelo Spinelli's family and
fiancée learned that he had been captured from this broadcast.

Kitchen where the soups were cooked for the American compound. Notice the ersatz coal in the buckets next to the large soup kettles. Morning coffee was also prepared in these kettles. Most of the men thought their morning coffee could be better used for shaving than for drinking.

Each barracks contained a stove for heat, but the prisoners could also cook simple things on it. The man on the left is peeling a very small potato while his buddy concocts a creative entrée.

EVEN WITH THE Red Cross parcels, we never really had enough to eat. I can remember digging around on the ground for just the smallest piece of bread. To this day, any waste of food galls me. Although we had little, the Russian prisoners had less. Sometimes we threw food over the fence to them.[8] In fact, I took a picture of a Russian POW in the adjacent compound who was shot and killed when he crawled too close to the danger zone between the fences while trying to retrieve a cigarette *(see photo, p. 6)*.

Thoughts of food could drive you crazy. I heard the story of an American commanding officer who was worried because his fellow prisoners were spending too much time talking about food. He thought it was damaging morale, so he suggested they talk about something else, like automobiles. "That's a good idea," said one of the prisoners. "Gosh, how I wish I had a shiny new auto—covered with mashed potatoes and gravy!"

We developed some very creative ways to cook our food. The guys made blower stoves out of old tin cans so we could get more heat out of the few pieces of wood, paper, or ersatz coal we managed to get. We cooked almost all our food parcels on these blowers. Some of the guys made a good living building these blowers for the other prisoners. They were paid off in food, chocolate bars, and cigarettes.

We also became very creative in how we prepared our food. Although I hope I never have to eat those dishes again, some of them would make Oscar of the Waldorf green with envy. I'll bet Oscar never used tooth powder instead of baking powder, nor made whipped cream out of powdered milk and margarine. And I'll wager he never thought of making ice cream out of snow, powdered milk, and jam. Maybe he'd like to try out this recipe for Kriegie pie à la mode:

Take a dozen C Ration crackers from the Red Cross food parcels, grind them up with a tin can grater, and then roll them into flour with a table leg rolling pin. Add two tablespoons of margarine, a tablespoon of powdered milk, eight tablespoons of water to form an excellent pie crust batter. Using one of the tin can pie tins, bake for four minutes in a tin can oven at what you hope is a moderate temperature. Boil the contents of either raisins or prunes from a food parcel and pour into pie crust. Bake this for another four minutes. Remove and cool and then take powdered milk, mix it into a very thick paste, spread over top, cut into eight pieces, and you have Kriegie pie à la mode.

Prisoners preparing to make pies with flour they bartered for with French POWs who had
access to German civilians because they worked outside the camp in the nearby town of
Fürstenberg.

As one can see in this photo, preparing dinner was a primitive undertaking before the prisoners developed their blower apparatuses for cooking their food *(see next page)*.

The blower left, built for Angelo Spinelli by a fellow POW, was a Rube Goldberg contraption constructed from old Red Cross cartons, empty cans, and sundry other items that could heat the evening meal with just a few chunks of ersatz coal. The frying pan on the right was made from a French water flask. Nothing was wasted. Two or more prisoners would share a blower.

According to Spinelli, next to food, the prisoners thought more about escape than anything else. The fact that most of these escapes existed in their imaginations rather than in reality did not really matter. This was good therapy, and dreaming of fleeing was much safer than joining the approximately one percent who actually did attempt an escape from a German prison camp. Spinelli also talks about a different kind of escape, one accomplished through attending formal classes, reading, playing sports, and attending or participating in the performing arts.

EVERY PRISONER dreamed of making a successful break for freedom. Many tried, but only one successfully escaped from Stalag IIIB. If any Kriegies got caught digging a tunnel, they were given thirty days of solitary confinement in the "cooler," and if they were caught in the tunnel they were lucky if they weren't shot by trigger-happy guards. One time the Kriegies got even by pouring water down a tunnel and nearly drowning the Germans who were worming their way through it.

The real escape for most prisoners was in reading books and going to educational classes. We had a camp library. The YMCA sent the books through the International Red Cross, and we made the shelving from Red Cross food parcel crates. I jotted down in a notebook the names of some of the books and magazines I requested and received from the International Red Cross in Geneva, and they covered everything from Italian grammar, to sociology, history, and photography. I even got Dante's *The Divine Comedy (see Appendix, p. 200)*.[9]

Our educational classes were taught by men who were experts in their respective fields in civilian life. One of the most popular courses in my camp was on salesmanship. The men liked the course so well they gave a party for their instructor at the end of it. When a man completed a course, he was given a certificate of completion, and records were kept to be sent to their school when the war ended. Unfortunately, almost all educational records were lost when the camps were evacuated in the last desperate days of the war. What some Kriegies did retain, however, were the rudimentary skills of the different trades that were taught in the camps.

The library in Stalag IIIB, which was housed in Barracks 17 of the American compound, contained over 10,000 volumes. These books came mostly from the International and American Red Cross and the YMCA. The shelves and desk were constructed by the prisoners, using Red Cross cartons.

Pursuing "The American Dream" in Stalag IIIB. The instructor of this popular course in salesmanship was fellow prisoner Fred Meachum, who had been a salesman in civilian life. The textbook (sent by the YMCA), was Paul W. Ivey's *Successful Salesmanship*, which had gone through several printings in the States during the late 1930s and 1940s. Those completing the course received a certificate.

Opposite: The prisoners in Stalag IIIB were able to take several formal classes, the most popular of which was a course in salesmanship. At the successful end of their "semester," the students honored their fellow prisoner/instructors with cakes they had bribed some French prisoners to make. The banner hanging from the table lists the attributes of a successful salesman:

Become Success Minded
Know Your Merchandise
Know Yourself—Develop Your Personality
Know the Customer
Appeal to Buying Motive
Plan the Sale
Get the Customer's Attention
Arouse Interest
Create Desire
Close the Sale—Use Correct Psychology
Close the Sale—Overcome Obstacles
Build Good Will

Angelo Spinelli's "Certificate" for completing fellow POW Fred L. Meachum's course in salesmanship.

WE ALSO PLAYED SPORTS, especially baseball. We had some former professional baseball players in our camp and some of the teams were very good. One of the stars was Mickey Grasso who later caught for the New York Giants. The YMCA provided athletic equipment, including baseball uniforms, bats, gloves, and balls, which the International Red Cross distributed to the camps.[10] The German guards became so interested in watching us play baseball that we got them to move the barbed wire fences back so we would have more room to play. We even had a marching band that played at some of the games. Of course, the barbed wire was rough on soccer balls and basketballs.

I almost got shot because of baseball. We were playing a game when the ball went over the warning wire. When I leaned over to pick it up, the guard in the tower shot at me. I saw a puff go up right in front of me as I bent down. It was a good thing I was bowlegged. The bullet went right through my trousers and in between my knees. I ran around the building so he couldn't get another shot.[11]

But baseball also saved me from spending a lengthy time in the cooler. If you got caught breaking the strict German regulations, the usual punishment was so many days in the cooler. It was a small structure, about four by eight feet, with just enough room to sleep. What happened was I was supposed to pitch for one of the teams in a Fourth of July baseball game. The day before I had sneaked over into the French compound to do some bartering, and I got caught. The guards immediately put me in the cooler. My first thought was, "Oh, oh. I can't pitch tomorrow." The next morning Lieutenant Gross was reading off the charges directed at those of us on report. Fortunately, during an earlier barracks' inspection, I took an American White Owl cigar my brother had sent me and stuffed it in his pocket. At the time, I thought this might help if I later got into trouble. So that morning he looked at me and then at his report and said, "This is the wrong number. Go back to your barracks." The cigar had worked, and I was able to pitch that day.

Baseball was a welcome diversion in Stalag IIIB, and the games were very well attended.
According to Tim Wolter, who wrote *POW Baseball in World War II*, "During the height of
the season there would be up to five games per day played on the athletic field . . . which
was also used for twice daily roll calls." Angelo Spinelli not only photographed the games but
also pitched for one of the teams.

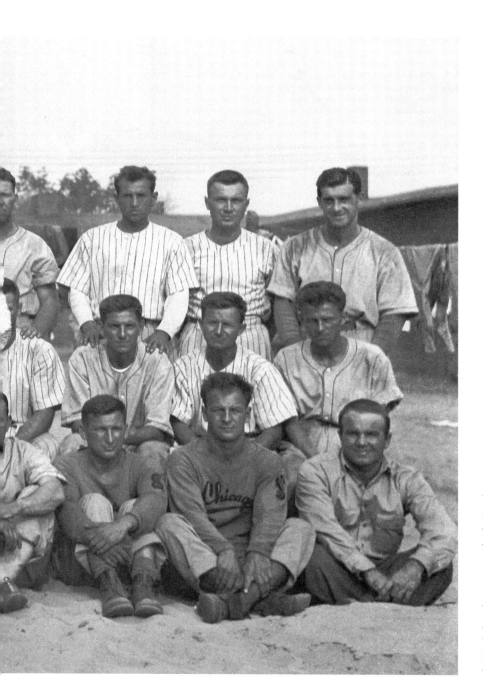

The ten baseball teams in Stalag IIIB played a regular schedule in one of two leagues: The Haudegen League featured the Indians, Rangers, Puddin' Heads, Zoot Suiters, Little Bears, and the Sharps. The Machorkow League included the Tigers, Nestle's Ten, Angel Faces, and Yanks. The YMCA donated a wide variety of athletic equipment, including uniforms that the men then tailored to their own liking.

Newton "Mickey" Grasso, who later played for the New York Giants and several other major league teams, taking his licks. Notice the large crowd, which often included many German guards and camp officials. The prisoners' barracks are in the background.

There was even a marching band in Stalag IIIB, shown here rehearsing for the opening of the baseball season. Band instruments were courtesy of the YMCA and the International Red Cross.

American prisoners playing touch football on a cold winter day in Stalag IIIB.

Using gloves furnished by the YMCA, two Americans square off in a boxing match in Stalag IIIB.

Although such fraternization was seldom allowed, French and American prisoners competed in this soccer match in Stalag IIIB.

Opposite: An American version of the German *Turnverein* (Gymnastics Club). Jack Mateur, who had been a gymnastics instructor back in Buffalo, New York, is the man on top.

IN ADDITION TO SPORTS, we also had a complete orchestra, with instruments provided by the YMCA. Many of the men had played professionally in civilian life, and when they put on one of their fine concerts, you forgot all about the barbed wire for a couple of hours.

We also put on plays, and especially musicals, with elaborate costumes and staging. Some of our sets were amazing. The men even built a revolving stage. And, for a play that featured a television broadcast, they made a stage built in sections on rollers so one scene after another could be shown on the "television screen."

The Germans gave us the equipment and tools we needed to put on our plays on what they called "parole." This meant that we could have them long enough to put on the play or build a stage set, but we had to return them every day. There was never a time that the German count didn't show something was missing, and then we'd have to go over everything with them to prove it was all there. Otherwise, we'd never get any equipment on parole again.

The plays became so popular, we had to issue tickets so that everyone would get a chance to see one of the five performances. However, some boys became such great theater fans that they became adept at counterfeiting our tickets—usually made from the tops of cheese boxes—and would see the same play five days in a row! Even some of the German guards would come and watch them.

Showbills

Time was clearly not important to these men and "women" who spent days building elaborate sets and constructing period costumes and wigs for their productions. This musical was called "Swing-Time." Notice London's Big Ben standing tall behind the car.

With or without talent, large numbers of prisoners in Stalag IIIB participated in the dramatic and musical presentations on a wide range of themes and characters. This is the cast from "Showboat."

The Chorus Line! Notice the footwear. The YMCA sent bowling shoes through the International Red Cross, but there were, of course, no bowling alleys in Stalag IIIB, or any other camp, so the "ladies" wore them for their dance numbers.

The Stalag IIIB Orchestra.

The American stage hands built this revolving stage for their productions.

The men built this elaborate pumpkin on a revolving stage for a gala Halloween show.
Musicians on the back side appeared as the stage revolved.

Vaudeville routines were always popular, such as this one set in New York City. The cigar-chomping store owner was played by Stanley Rubin. Lou Ambrose is to Rubin's immediate left. The policeman's name was Sorenson.

Years before television found its way into American living rooms, a prisoner who had worked for RCA crafted this futuristic set for one of Stalag IIIB's dramatic presentations.

A LOT OF THE MEN developed hobbies to keep their minds and hands busy. A man never knows what he can do until he has to do it. To keep from losing our minds, many a Kriegie became proficient in building model airplanes, doing watercolors or oil paintings, or even making a clock from tin cans. Some handicrafts took a very practical turn. Men became experts in repairing shoes. Others cut hair or became tailors and repaired uniforms and made stage costumes. Some became bookbinders and gave new life to our well-used volumes. Still others took up watch repairing and did themselves and their fellow prisoners a good turn by keeping our watches running. In addition to my photography, I did a series of pen and ink sketches, only a couple of which I was able to bring home with me.

Pen and ink sketches by Angelo Spinelli.

Using tools donated by the YMCA and the International Red Cross, prisoners busy themselves with a watch repair service located in the camp library.

Haircuts could be obtained free from friends or for a couple of cigarettes from a "professional" barber. In this shot, Roland La Pointe is administering to Pipes Gaskin. The blankets and clothes in the background are being aired in the hope of eliminating various vermin.

This unidentified American POW was in charge of designing the many stage settings for Stalag IIIB's numerous plays and musical productions. For his office, he used the washroom located between the chapel and the theater in Barracks 17.

Also using the washroom in Barracks 17 for a studio were the camp's various artists, including Angelo Spinelli who drew his pen and ink sketches there. Notice the water pipes, covered to prevent freezing in winter.

Using materials furnished by the YMCA or the International Red Cross, an unidentified American prisoner painted this portrait of Lou Boettcher, the American band leader in Stalag IIIB.

A LIGHTER SIDE of POW life was the slang that emerged in the camps. Dehydrated vegetable soup was "green death" or "seaweed." A big meal or a party was a "bash," and a Kriegie with an uncontrollable appetite was a "bashomaniac." A prisoner became "browned-off" or "Kriegie-happy" from being too long in captivity. Anything that was wrong or stupid was "from hunger" because your mind is not sharp when food is scarce. A prisoner "strictly from hunger" was something of a jerk, or a sad sack.

All this may sound like we were having lots of fun, and many of my photos certainly do show GIs smiling and playing ball or putting on plays and concerts. We may look like we were having a good time, but all this was just a shield to keep us from going into a complete depression. When a prisoner allowed this to happen, there was no way out of it. What could he do? Some guys had to be restrained, and some did commit suicide. Why? Because the future looked so bleak. You had to guard against yourself thinking, "I didn't do anything wrong. Why is this happening to me? Why am I suffering so?" Some of the more sadistic guards said they were going to kill us. And for a long time we didn't get any news about us winning the war, so we had to find ways to occupy our time and keep up our morale. There were long discussions and arguments on any subject we could dream up. We could also spend an hour and a half just fixing our evening meal. If you had a piece of bread or some simple item of food, you could take a long time getting a fire going and heating it. Some guys spent hours making those blower stoves from scraps of wood and tin cans that we used to heat up or cook our food. Others would spend days preparing to put on a light-hearted play or become involved in a wide variety of crafts. Some loved to sunbathe, when the weather permitted, whereas others were avid walkers, who every day strolled miles around the compound. Then there were those who just lay on their beds, staring at the ceiling or stood quietly outside, counting the barbs on the fence, or gazing aimlessly into space.

Overleaf: Boredom and inertia could adversely affect a prisoner's will to survive every bit as much as did hunger, sickness, and cold. It was important to fill the long, empty hours, lest one fall into what some POWs referred to as "barbed-wire psychosis."

The winter of 1944–1945 was one of the coldest in German history. Fortunately, most of the men in this photo had overcoats. Footwear, however, was always a problem, especially if all you had were standard-issue U.S. Army leather boots.

Opposite: American POW Lou Singer from New York makes the cold, lonely trek back to his barracks from the latrine building in the background. When one was afflicted with dysentery or diarrhea, as so many of the prisoners were, this was a painful and frequent walk.

Angelo Spinelli does not remember this prisoner's name, although he does recall he was from Iowa, was housed in Barracks 19B, and drew many caricatures of Spinelli trading with his German captors. Unfortunately, none of these drawings survived captivity.

On warm, sunny days, POWs would shed their clothes and sunbathe. They also hoped the fresh air would help rid their blankets, clothes, and bodies of ticks, fleas, lice, and mouse droppings. Notice how much cleaner the sand is where the men are lying than in the background. They had turned the sand over to bury the surface grime.

Prisoners watching a stalled German armored vehicle along the Oder Canal.
Because of the threat of air attacks, POW camps were not supposed to be located
near military forces or equipment.

Whenever a German woman walked along the canal, the prisoners would line up and throw Red Cross cigarettes and other items to attract her attention. Professional baseball player Mickey Grasso could always hit a raised skirt with a package of Lucky Strikes.

IT WAS SO IMPORTANT to keep your mind occupied, but even the best of us had those moments when everything seemed to shut down, and we became depressed about the uncertainty that was always with us. When these dark moments occurred, many of us called on our religious faith to keep us going. We often did this as individuals, but we also built a chapel where we could worship together. Using pieces of wood from Red Cross parcels, broken glass, and almost anything else we could find, we constructed our house of worship in Barracks 17. One prisoner even made a mural for the chapel, using pieces of glass. The YMCA sent us a wide variety of religious items we could use in our services, which were conducted for all faiths. We kept the chapel open all during the day, so any time you got depressed, you could go in and say a prayer, which always made me feel better.

For our Sunday services, we Catholics had a Polish priest who said mass. He must have been a prisoner but I'm not sure about his background. He brought his own chalice, and we did have communion, but I don't remember having confession. The Protestant services were conducted by an American prisoner who later became a chaplain.

It was my faith in God, along with my picture-taking, that kept me going, especially in those darkest moments when I thought I might not make it. But even when the guards threatened me, I would say to myself, "The Lord is more powerful than they are." Without this kind of faith, I might have given up. I still have the rosary I bartered for from another POW. It was beautifully crafted from bits of wire and beads made from fragments of the Plexiglas cockpit of a shot-down airplane.

Using scraps from Red Cross parcels, pieces of glass, and religious items sent by the YMCA, the prisoners in Stalag IIIB constructed this chapel in Barracks 17, which also contained the library and the theater. Regular services were held for all faiths. Frank Stebbing, who was the editor of the prison newspaper, the *POW-WOW*, was so moved by the chapel he wrote the poem, "The Honest Prayer of Lonely Men."

The Honest Prayer of Lonely Men
by Frank Stebbing[12]

There was no temple for our Lord
When we were banished to this place
Of soldier-exile. Yet we saw
Within the barbs His lonely face.

So we saved up the precious wood
Of crates from home, and scraps of tin,
And built on sands of solitude
A House where God might enter in.

And wealthy men on golden hills,
And men despoiled by luxury's kiss
Have never a temple for their Lord
As beautiful and true as this.

God loves the wealth of barren spots,
And we are not the less His own
Because when Jesus enters in
We seat Him on a humble throne.

For He, impatient when His ear
Has caught the plea of princely sin,
Whispers: "Wait! While first I hear
The honest prayer of lonely men!"

Angelo Spinelli paid a fellow American POW two packs of cigarettes to make this rosary.
The artist cut the beads from the Plexiglas cockpit of a shot-down airplane and obtained the
crucifix from a French prisoner for a pack of cigarettes.

Another shot of the chapel that meant so much to Angelo Spinelli and many of his fellow prisoners. The piano was donated by the YMCA and transported to Stalag IIIB by the International Red Cross. The benches were brought in from the barracks for Sunday services and for evening plays and concerts.

Paintings by an unknown American POW
in Stalag IIIB.

A mosaic made from pieces of glass by an unknown artist.

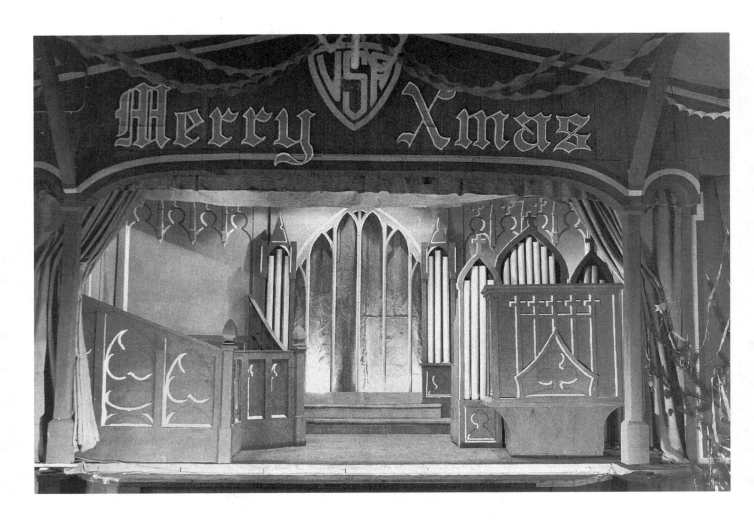

The American compound's chapel decorated for Christmas 1944.

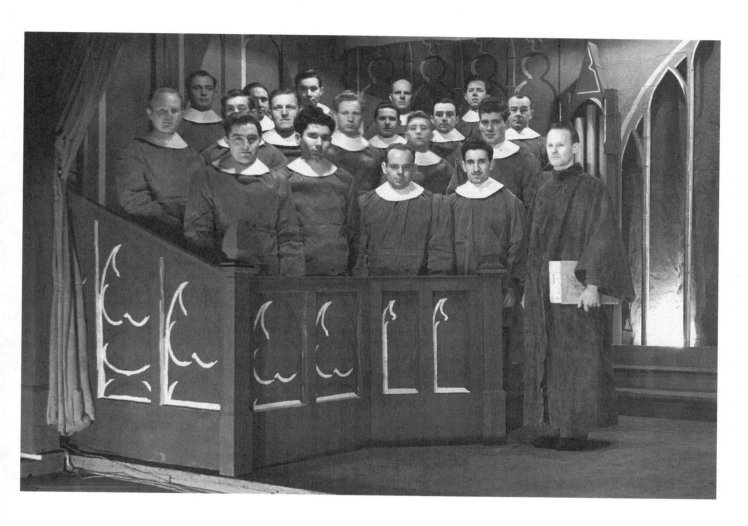

Wearing gowns they sewed themselves, the American POW choir rehearsing for its Christmas program in Stalag IIIB. Russell Hehr was the choirmaster. Angelo Spinelli used his tripod for this shot and a 9-second time exposure with the smallest diaphragm opening to get the desired depth.

With the acquisition of his camera, Spinelli regained a sense of mission that helped counter any feelings of tedium and depression. When the first Red Cross parcels arrived in Stalag IIIB in the summer of 1943, Spinelli had the means to acquire his camera.

IT WAS PROBABLY July or August of 1943 before we began getting Red Cross parcels. In addition to providing us additional food that we so desperately needed, the Red Cross parcels allowed us to trade with each other and even to bribe the guards. I did a lot of both.

We used Red Cross items such as chocolate bars and especially cigarettes to trade with the guards. We traded these for additional food, like real bread from the nearby village, and, eventually, for all kinds of things. Trading with the guards became so well established in our camp, we even had a price list. A typical list of prices even appeared in our camp newspaper, the *POW-WOW*, on June 25, 1943:

O.D. Shirt	*2 cigarettes*
Br. Blouse	*2 cigarettes*
W. Undershirt	*1½ cigarettes*
W. Drawers	*1½ cigarettes*
C. Undershirt	*1 cigarette*
C. Shorts	*1 cigarette*
Face towel	*1 cigarette*
Field Jacket	*3 cigarettes*
Combat pants	*3 cigarettes*

Cigarettes were the most valuable thing a POW could have. Almost all the Americans smoked. Some guys even gave up their much needed food to get cigarettes. Fortunately, I did not smoke. If I had, I never would have had been able to get my camera and film.

Even before I got to IIIB, I had accumulated quite a storehouse of cigarettes. The night before we left Stalag 7A at Moosburg, I got into a card game and won a lot of script money, which the Germans issued to the guys who went on work details.[13] After we arrived in IIIB, I used this script to buy German cigarettes. Then I told the guys I would give them two German cigarettes for one American cigarette when and if we ever got our Red Cross parcels. When the parcels came in, I had a list of all the fellows who owed me American cigarettes. After I collected these, I had a nice accumulation for trading purposes.

I also wrote home saying, "Please send me lots of cigars and cigarettes because I'm just as heavy a smoker as I was at home." My family figured out that I was using tobacco for barter. Cigars were unique, and my brother sent two or three boxes, some of which actually got through to me *(for examples of the cards and letters Spinelli sent home, see Appendix, pp. 191–95).*

It was truly amazing that Angelo Spinelli's secret photographs were never discovered by the German camp officials. Certainly several of his fellow prisoners knew about his camera, but no one ever informed on him. Ed La Porta, who would save Spinelli's life on the forced march from IIIB to IIIA, reported that some of Spinelli's fellow prisoners were suspicious of him and his camera because they thought he might be working for the Germans. La Porta said he and those who knew better assured the others that this was certainly not the case.[14] Joe DiMare, who also realized that Spinelli's camera raised fears among his fellow prisoners, later wrote, "There were those who thought Spinelli, with his camera, might be drawing the German 'ire' on us since the camera, as a tool of the spy and saboteur was 'verboten' and if caught was punishable at the commandant's discretion in addition to inviting 'shakedowns' looking for such things as arms, radios, and cameras."[15] But others, such as Burdette Parrott, who lived in Barracks 19A with Spinelli, found him to be very much the loner, not letting anyone get too close to him. Parrott does remember Spinelli always wearing his baggy paratrooper trousers, but insisted he had no idea that he was hiding his camera in them.[16]

After finding out which guards were willing to barter, it took me a couple of months to get one guard's confidence, but once I did, I used him for the remainder of the time I was there. He was in his sixties and insisted he was not a Nazi. He had lost his entire family in the bombing of Berlin and didn't care whether he lived or not.

I traded him eight packs of cigarettes for a 120mm, folding-bellows Voightlander Bessa camera. The camera was about three by eight inches and a little over an inch thick. I gave this same guard one pack of cigarettes to get me a roll of film and another pack to get it developed. He probably gave four or five cigarettes to the man in town who processed the roll. There were times when I had as many as thirty rolls of film, but I would only give the guard one roll at a time for processing because I feared it might never come back.

Spinelli's Voightlander Bessa camera.

I later swapped two or three packs of cigarettes for a folding tripod that opened to about five feet and closed to some eight inches. I used the tripod for indoor shots and exposure times of eight to twelve seconds in case it was a slow-speed film. I had no flash attachment. I also traded cigarettes for a pair of paratrooper pants, which I wore when I wanted to walk around the compound and take pictures. I tied a string to the camera and lowered it down into these baggy pants. Then I could just pull the camera up to about my waist, look down into the viewfinder, press the lens release on the folding apparatus, and start shooting. I would hide in the shadows and wait for the guards to turn their backs. Occasionally, when I sneaked into a forbidden area to take pictures, I would use a trustworthy buddy as a lookout. But most of the guys didn't know I was taking these pictures. I had to be careful because one of them might have told somebody else that I had a camera, and it would have eventually got back to the Germans.

I also never told the other POWs I was getting my film processed because word would get around, and they would try it and get caught. A few of the other POWs had cameras, but they never were able to develop their film. I don't know what they did with it. They also did not know what to take. They'd take pictures of their friends. I did that too, but more important were the pictures I took of what was going on in the camp.

I kept my negatives hidden in a little box I buried under the bedpost of my bunk in Barracks 19B. I made this box out of wood taken from a Red Cross parcel and sealed it with soap so it wouldn't leak. Then I made a concrete lid to fit over the top. I got the cement for

French prisoners building a doorway in the barracks 17 which contained the theater, library, and chapel. Spinelli managed to "requisition" a bag of cement from them to build the concrete lid, under which he hid his camera, film, and tripod.

some cigarettes I swapped with a French prisoner who was making a doorway to the library.

Overall, I probably took more than 1,000 shots, but some weren't exposed properly and sometimes the film itself was bad. There was nothing I could do about that. Because I couldn't read German, I had to guess at the settings and shutter speeds. I just took pictures with what I had. I destroyed the negatives that weren't good and kept only the printable ones in the box.

The interior of Angelo Spinelli's Barracks 19B. One side of the barracks contained triple-decker bunks; on the other side were tables and benches. There was a single washroom containing eight cold water spigots in between. At each end there was a urinal that often overflowed. The major latrine was in a separate building at the back of the compound. When Spinelli took this shot, the other prisoners were outside for roll call. At the back right, Frank Palari is serving as a lookout.

This is the only photo of Angelo Spinelli wearing the baggy paratrooper pants inside of which he suspended his hidden camera on a string. A trusted buddy took this posed shot of Spinelli reading his prayer book and a letter from home.

I NEVER TOOK ANY photos of the guard who got me the camera and processed the film for the same reason I never kept a diary. In our camp the authorities insisted on examining everything. If a particular item was all right, they would stamp it *Geprüft*, which means "examined." One of our guys made a stamp out of a rubber heel that we then used to stamp *Geprüft* on all kinds of pictures, like the ones the guys got from home, so if a guard saw one, he wouldn't know where it came from—it was just *Geprüft*. But I didn't want to take any such chances with my pictures.[17]

There was always danger, but that only made me all the more determined to take these photos. I thought to myself, "If by chance these pictures get back to the States, the American people will find out how we kept body and soul together and how we kept from going crazy or committing suicide."

If the film processor would have snitched to the SS or if the SS would have gotten hold of the pictures, it would have been curtains for everybody involved. In a way, this fear of death was liberating. Since we thought we were going to die anyway, we were willing to take risks. At the time, I wasn't afraid. I'm more afraid now when I think back on it.

With all the shakedowns by the SS troops, as well as by the regular German soldiers, it's a wonder that more of us didn't get caught. Usually, one of the guards the GIs were trading with would alert us. The guards were also afraid of these inspections. If one of us had been caught with something we were not supposed to have and said, "Oh, the guard got that for me," the guard would have been immediately sent to the Eastern Front, which was an almost certain death sentence.

One time during an *SS* shakedown, I realized I had some developed film in my pocket that my guard had just brought back from the village. I started shaking like a leaf. There was an announcement over the camp loudspeaker that all prisoners were to line up for an inspection. Several were randomly selected for a full strip search, but fortunately I was not one of them. We always feared the *SS*.

Imagine what might have happened to all concerned if the German *Kommandant* had discovered that Angelo Spinelli had taken a photograph of two prisoners trading with a guard. Lou Ambrose is the prisoner in the forefront who is offering a can of Red Cross margarine for a kilo of non-ersatz German bread. German civilian bread usually contained a lesser percentage of bark and sawdust than did the bread the POWs received in camp.

148

American POW Joe Lombardo offers the guard a cigarette to allow him to enter the French compound to barter for food. Lombardo was dressed in French clothes to fool any other Germans who might encounter him after he left the American compound. The French prisoners were compelled to work in the nearby town where they could often steal or trade for food. According to the Geneva Convention, because they were NCOs, the American POWs in Stalag IIIB could not be forced to work, although they could volunteer to do so.

French POWs digging an air raid trench in the American compound of Stalag IIIB.

Spinelli took this remarkable shot looking across the wire into the Russian compound where the Russian prisoners were waiting to be counted. American prisoners occasionally threw food and cigarettes over this fence, sometimes in exchange for handmade trinkets and sometimes simply because they wanted to help their Russian counterparts survive. According to Spinelli, "When a Russian died, the others would stand him up at roll call so they could get his rations."

Two factors dictated the abysmal conditions and deadly fate of the Russian prisoners. Beginning with its leaders, most Germans had utter contempt for Russians. Hitler referred to them as "Mongol Half-Wits" and told his armed forces, "This enemy consists not of soldiers but to a large extent only of beasts." Soviet Premier Josef Stalin also helped seal the fate of his own prisoners. He totally rejected those who had apparently allowed themselves to become prisoners, and his refusal to sign the 1929 Geneva Accord meant Russian prisoners had no access to Red Cross parcels or international guarantees of decent treatment. As a result, more than three million Russian prisoners died in German captivity.

STALAG IIIA — LUCKENWALDE

On January 31, 1945, with Russian troops closing in, the German officers, with little warning, ordered their prisoners to evacuate Stalag IIIB. Their departure was so hasty that the prisoners were provided with no provisions and had nothing to eat on the forced march except a few pieces of bread. Water was in equally short supply. Not surprisingly, under such conditions many of the prisoners, including Angelo Spinelli, became sick before reaching Stalag IIIA at Luckenwalde on February 7, 1945. Spinelli remembers little of the march except that two buddies saved his life.

WE HAD NO ADVANCED warning before we were ordered to move out of IIIB. I had to leave a lot behind, but I was able to stuff my prayer book and rosary, some pictures from home, a small notebook, my razor and toothbrush, and, above all, my camera and negatives into my musette bag. I carried a little food and some clothing separately. We marched through snow and slush for hours that first night, and I got sicker and sicker. Finally, I just couldn't go any farther. I fell to the ground and couldn't get up. I thought to myself, "Hell, I can't go on. I don't care if they shoot me. I just don't care anymore." But once more, the good Lord was watching over me, and these two buddies, Ed La Porta and James Everett, picked me up and put me and my precious possessions on this German wagon. There's no question I would have been shot if they hadn't helped me.

Ed La Porta, who was trying to help another sick prisoner on the march, remembered years later how he had jeopardized his own life by helping Spinelli: "I was carrying Gearinger on my back. I could see Spinelli walking, but I could tell he was getting weak. I thought to myself, 'Oh my God, now I've also got Spinelli to worry about.' Then Spinelli fell down. So I put down Gearinger for a moment and walked over and asked Spinelli what the matter was. He told me, 'I can't make it. I just can't go any further.' Just about that time this horse-drawn wagon with a German driver came along. So I picked up Spinelli and put him on the wagon. That German driver never turned around and never said a word; he just kept on going. I took a big chance to stop and pick up Spinelli. If the German guards had noticed me doing that, Spinelli would have been shot and probably I would have too."[18]

Each night the German soldier who was driving this wagon would stop at the local village police station where we would sleep. He kept telling us to look very sick so that the wagon wouldn't be taken away, and he would have to walk with us the rest of the way.

A half century passed before I saw either Jim Everett or Ed La Porta again. Much to my surprise, on April 9, 2000, Ed La Porta came to the opening of my photographic exhibit at the Andersonville POW Museum. About five years ago I met Jim Everett at a national POW convention. He told me it had cost him four Chesterfield cigarettes to get me on that wagon, which was the first I had heard about this. Imagine, without his cigarettes neither my precious photographs nor I would have made it. So it's only been during the past few years that I have had the chance to properly thank these two men for saving my life.

✪

By the time we got to Stalag IIIA, I had lost or thrown away almost everything, even a notebook of drawings I had made that I worked on for several months. I did manage to save two of these sketches *(see p. 107)*. Above all, I was determined not to throw away my camera and negatives, which were still in my musette bag. I also had my overcoat and a few other articles of clothing.

We immediately had a shakedown inspection, but I had time to observe the prisoners being inspected in front of me. When I came up to this long table where they were doing the inspecting, I was ordered to put everything on the table. I put my coat and the other personal things on the table, but I held my musette bag by its strap suspended out of sight under the table. I immediately put a pack of cigarettes in the hand of the guard, and when he quickly shoved me forward, I dragged my musette bag along the edge of the table. When I got to another guard at the end of the table, I took another package of cigarettes out of my pocket and put it into the palm of his hand. Then I put on my coat and other things, which had been on the table over the musette bag, and walked out.

From the day we arrived at Stalag IIIA until we were liberated by the Russian troops and tanks on their way to fight the Battle of Berlin, we never had another shakedown. Had there been any kind of search, I would have been in great trouble because I had no place to hide anything in IIIA. Without a doubt, the Germans would have found my camera and negatives, and I might have been shot, especially if they had turned me over to the *SS*. So I was constantly worried for the three months I was in Luckenwalde. Living conditions were also much worse than they had been in IIIB, particularly because of the overcrowding and the lack of sanitary facilities. And because the Red Cross parcels no longer were able to reach us with any regularity, we had very little to eat. I was down to 115 pounds when the Russians liberated us on April 22, 1945.

The only really beautiful thing I saw in Stalag IIIA was the Russian chapel, which I photographed shortly after liberation. I have no idea where the Russian prisoners got the materials, but the chapel was filled with beautiful works of art.

Angelo Spinelli took this shot of the Russian chapel in Stalag IIIA just after liberation. Because conditions were so much worse for Russian prisoners, Spinelli was amazed to see their chapel filled with magnificent paintings, wood carvings, mosaics, and tapestries.

157

Images from the Russian Chapel in Stalag IIIA.

LIBERATION AND HOME

AFTER THE RUSSIANS rolled into Stalag IIIA on April 22, 1945, there was total chaos. Most of the guards had fled or been killed by the Russians, so we just wandered around, both inside and outside the camp, wondering how we were going to get back to the American lines. I had used up all the 120mm film for my Voightlander camera, but I was able to get some 35mm film, and my buddy Roland Chathum, who had also been a combat photographer, and I managed to get a new camera. We were walking through a field and came across a German plane that had been shot down. Roland knew there was a 35mm camera in the wing so we took it out, and I took pictures with this Robat camera all the way back to the States.[19]

After a few days, a convoy of ambulances arrived in IIIA to pick up the sick. Just before the ambulances left, five French prisoners, including one I had previously traded with, stole a German truck. Roland and I climbed on the truck and followed the ambulances back to the American lines.

Liberation Day, April 22, 1945!

Russian troops liberating Stalag IIIA.

After Russian troops, trucks, and tanks liberated Stalag IIIA at Luckenwalde on the morning of April 22, 1945, they quickly moved on to the Battle of Berlin, leaving the prisoners on their own. Not a German to be found anywhere. They had either fled or been killed by the Russians. The sign on the barracks reads *Lager Kantine*. This was the camp commissary where POWs could spend their *Lager Geld* on various items. This camp money, in accordance with the 1929 Geneva Accord, was earned by working outside the camps. Because officers were not allowed to work, and NCOs only if they volunteered, such money was earned mostly by enlisted men.

Confusion reigned after the Russians liberated Camp IIIA. Some of the prisoners just waited; others, like Spinelli, struck out for the American lines to the west. The two rows of wire on the right separated the compounds. The space between the two wires was "no man's land" where, before liberation, trespassers could be shot.

After liberation, the prisoners waiting for transportation still had to eat. Roland Chatham, who helped Angelo Spinelli procure his second camera shortly after liberation, and Joe Castellano are cooking on an abandoned German wagon. The guards had taken the horse when they fled the night before the Russians arrived.

After liberation, U.S. Army ambulances transported those prisoners too sick to walk back to
the American lines.

Opposite: Several former French prisoners commandeered a truck which they planned to
drive home to France. After taking their picture, Spinelli hitched a ride with them as far as
the American lines.

WHEN WE GOT BACK to the American front lines, Roland and I jumped off the truck and identified ourselves. We asked the MPs if there was a communications unit in the vicinity. Sure enough, there was, and they put us up and fed us. The officer in charge tried to get us transportation on a plane back to the States, but we had to follow normal procedures with the other liberated prisoners. We were then flown to Paris and transported by land to Camp Lucky Strike at Le Havre, which was the staging area for POWs returning to the States.

After we got on the ship home, I spent almost the entire time in the ship's hospital. I had constant pain in my back, and I couldn't stand for any length of time. While I was in the ship's sick bay, I could not remember where my musette bag was, with all my cameras and negatives, and, quite frankly, at that point I really didn't care. Luckily, nothing was stolen. Just before we landed in New York on June 13, 1945, one of the hospital attendants called me in and handed me all my belongings, including my cameras and pictures. Nothing was missing, and I was able to take a couple of final photographs of us coming into the harbor.

Using the camera he and Roland Chatham took from a downed German fighter plane, Spinelli took this shot of the C-47s that flew him and other liberated POWs from Germany to Paris.

The "Wash-Tent" at Camp Lucky Strike near Le Havre, France, where the men gathered before boarding ships for the United States. According to Spinelli, the former prisoners spent all day eating, trying to recover some of the weight they had lost in the German prison camps.

Even after liberation, Angelo Spinelli and his camera continued to chronicle the unusual. This warning sign appeared in Camp Lucky Strike in northern France, where American soldiers waited for transportation home.

Land Ahoy! Steaming into New York Harbor.

Opposite: Landing in New York! The sign on shores says, "Welcome Home. Well Done."

CIVILIAN SPINELLI AND HIS PHOTOGRAPHS

After landing in New York, Angelo Spinelli spent a few days in a military hospital before being granted a seventy-four-day furlough, after which he received his honorable discharge on September 22, 1945. On July 29, he married Anna Egidio, who had faithfully waited for him for four long years. He also joined his brother Joseph in launching the Spinl Jewelry Company of New York City, which specialized in the manufacturing and sale of bracelets and rings. Shortly before his marriage, Spinelli attended a special luncheon hosted by the New York YMCA to celebrate the safe return of area POWs. It was an event that would eventually change his life.

THE FIRST PEOPLE to see my photographs in the United States were representatives of the New York YMCA. On July 23, 1945, they threw a benefit for all former POWs who were from the metropolitan area. That's where I met John Burkhart, who was the Manager for Public Relations for the YMCA nationwide. I told him, "Hey, I've got photographs I took of POW life in Germany."

He didn't believe me and asked, "What kind of pictures could you possibly have?"

I told him, "You'd be surprised what I've got."

I finally convinced Burkhart and we made an appointment. After I showed him my negatives, he took them and made 8 x 10 prints for me. I asked him if we needed clearance from military authorities, but he told me, "Don't worry, that's all taken care of." I later found out that the army had no rights to my photos because they had not been taken with military equipment.

Burkhart and his colleagues at the YMCA were so impressed with my photos that they put together and published 50,000 copies of a booklet entitled *The Yankee Kriegies*. The majority of the photographs in it are mine. It also contains numerous prints of Col. C. Ross Greening's watercolor paintings of prison life. The YMCA then sponsored a traveling exhibit. Unfortunately, I was already back working so I didn't have the time to accompany the exhibit, but Colonel Greening traveled across the country with it, talking about his experiences and paintings and giving away copies of *The Yankee Kriegie*.

Others were not initially as captivated by Angelo Spinelli's photographs as the YMCA had been. The U.S. Army expressed no interest, nor did the Time-Life Corporation, the best known source of news photos in the country.

Across the street from the YMCA's New York headquarters was the Time-Life Building. I went to their offices to see if they might be interested in my photographs. An editor took a number of my prints and told me he'd get right back to me. When he didn't, I pestered him constantly for maybe four weeks. When he still did nothing, I got annoyed and told him, "You obviously don't want to produce my pictures, so the hell with you. Give them back to me." He did, and I put them away in my office where they stayed for the next thirty-three years.

After the Time-Life disappointment, I just clammed up about my POW experiences. I wouldn't talk about them to anybody. It's something you feel inside that's hard to describe. I didn't even talk to my family because they could not really understand what we had to do to survive when we were so cold and hungry. I suppose I also felt guilty. First there was the guilt of having been captured. You are not supposed to be taken prisoner. Then there was the guilt of having survived when so many others did not. It took a long time before I started talking, and even then the only ones who really understood were other POWs.

Several things got me to open up. Attending POW reunions helped, and after the American hostages in Iran were released in 1980, therapy sessions for ex-POWs became more common, and we were encouraged to talk about our experiences. Then, too, after Time-Life decided the second time around to publish some of my photographs, a lot of people began contacting me about my pictures. Today it no longer bothers me to talk about my twenty-six months as a prisoner, but there are still certain memories that choke me up.

IN 1979, A DIFFERENT Time-Life editor found my photos from *The Yankee Kriegie* in the Library of Congress. He called me from Virginia and asked if I were the same Angelo Spinelli who took those photographs. I told him I certainly was. He then made arrangements for someone from the New York office to take a look at my photo collection. The editor who came to the house was amazed. As a result, in 1981 Time-Life used many of my pictures, plus some of its own, in its *Prisoners of War: World War II*, which was a volume in its *Victory in Europe* series. Six double pages of my photographs appear in both the English and German language editions. Naturally, this exposure brought renewed interest in my pictures. Now all kinds of individuals and organizations wanted them.

✪

I DONATED SOME of my prints to Yale University, the Air Force Museum, the U.S. Army Signal Corps, and the U.S. Army Military History Institute, but they all wanted me to donate my negatives. I told the military museums, "Get me the Medal of Honor, and the negatives are yours." I firmly believed my photographs were worthy of that kind of recognition. They asked me if I could get an officer to testify to what I had done. I told them, "I don't need anyone to testify. The pictures speak for themselves."

On June 5, 2000, I decided to donate my 400 negatives, my two cameras, and my tripod to the National POW Museum at the Andersonville National Historic Site in Georgia, and that's where they will remain. Fred Sanchez, who is the Chief Ranger at the Andersonville Historic Site, was the smartest of all those trying to get my negatives. He asked me to send him some negatives so he could preserve them on computer disks. So I sent him about a dozen. He sent me a copy of the disk, and then asked me to send more negatives. He wanted to put together an exhibit of my photos, and I agreed. This cost them thousands of dollars. I figured if they were willing to spend that kind of money, and because it's our national prisoner of war museum, I should give them my entire collection. Besides, Andersonville is the one place that honors all POWs.

✪

WHAT I DID is part of history. People may forget me, but my pictures will always be in the Andersonville National Historic Site. After all of us POWs are dead and gone, those photographs will still be there. This makes me feel so good. No amount of dollars could ever give me such a feeling. I don't need any money. I have my burial plot already paid for. So I have no financial worries. I'm just happy I was able to do it.

A few voices have criticized my photos because some of them seem to create a sense of enjoyment and pleasure. This is far from the truth. A day did not go by that each and everyone of us POWs did not fear we might be assembled and summarily executed.[20] Several prisoners went stir crazy, and even willed themselves to death, because they could not cope with life in the camps. It was my constant belief in God and prayer that helped me to cope and to believe that my life would be spared. And if I didn't make it, I hoped that in some way, someone would discover my photos and have visible proof as to how we lived behind barbed wire. Of course, I can never forget my own memories of having been a POW. I learned that freedom is priceless. Only after it had been taken away, did I realize what it meant to be a free and independent human being.

On June 5, 2000, Angelo Spinelli donated his entire World War II photographic collection to the National Prisoner of War Museum in Andersonville, Georgia.

APPENDIX

This is the only surviving copy of Stalag IIIB's POW newspaper, *The POW-WOW,* from June 25, 1943. Former German camp officer F. W. Von Fricken gave it to Angelo Spinelli when they renewed their friendship in New Jersey in 1986. In the lower right corner is a "Best Wishes" greeting to Von Fricken from "The Staff."

THE *POW-WOW*: STALAG IIIB'S POW NEWSPAPER

POW-WOW Staff

Frank Stebbing	Editor-in-Chief
"Pop" Dimmic	Associate Editor
"Ade" Mersfelder	Art Editor
Carl Gerhard	Managing Editor
Bob Royster	Camp Relations
Joe Bush	Sports Editor
Ed Eltife	Publicity

Contributing Writers

Beau Fonda	Dick Gray
Bill Pinto	George Strawser
Bernie Hartman	Bill Freund

Barracks Reporters

No. 13	Mitchell Dennison
No. 14	Bob Royster
No. 15	Abe Freeman
No. 16	Tom Maston
No. 18	Dave Speakman
No. 19	Dick Behrens
No. 20	Bob King

Chapel Chimes
Protestant
by Dick Gray and Bob Berger

Scripture Lesson for the Week—St. Luke, 6:40–44

Our church is showing great progress. Both Protestant and Catholic services become larger and more impressive each week. The combined sect church committee is working hard to give the fellows services as much like those at home as possible. We need your help. We can build the "outer chapel," but it will take you men to build the "inner church." So come to the service of your choice, and let's try to build a strong Christian fellowship we would all like to find in our home churches. Even though our crowds are large, there are still many faces missing. We are expecting to have a special service Sunday, so why not everyone come and make it truly a service to be remembered?

Protestant Services: 9 a.m.
Message: "Fox Hole Atheist," by Cpl. Beckendorf
Choir Specialty: "Sweet Bye and Bye"
Congregational hymns assisted by Brass Ensemble

Chapel Chimes
Catholic
by John J. Pacholec

What Is the Mass?

Your Sunday Mass is the climax on earth of God's search for you and your search for God, beginning with interior prayer and leading to exterior sacrifice. Our personal prayers and sacrifices are incomplete without Jesus; hence, the absolute necessity of your attending Sunday Mass. Time is something we have plenty of, and an hour spent each week hearing Mass will not inconvenience anyone. At Mass, we adore God, because He is supreme, thank Him for all gifts we have received. . . .

Catholic Mass Barracks 17B
10:00 a.m. High Mass, French Padre officiating, assisted by Choir.
Priest will give General Absolution
Choir will rehearse every morning at 9 a.m. in Barracks 17B

The Three R's
by Bernie Hartman

How many of you men are interested in the fundamentals of Economics and English? I know there are many of you scattered throughout this Compound who are looking for an opportunity of this kind. Now, let's get together and come on over to Barracks 13A. Every morning at 8, except Sundays, the Economics Class meets. At 2 p.m., Monday through Friday, is the time for English.

We want *more* men in these classes. Do not feel, because we have already started, that you should not come. We plan a reorganization just as soon as the rest of you come, and possibilities of actual classrooms are in the offing, with a wide curriculum.

The Bookworm

The familiar cry for the past week has been: "When's the library going to open?" Well, the official opening date will be June 28th. More news as to regulations governing the library will be issued to each barracks some time this week. There's a variety of books here, such as Mystery, Crime, Romance, Western, and Travels . . . by familiar authors such as Wm. Saroyan, Ellery Queen, J. J. Van Dine, P. G. Wodehouse, Ed. Gardner, and many others. For the conservative reader, there are books by Poe, Shelley, Shakespeare, Burns, Milton, Byron, Tennyson, and, of course, Charles Dickens. But come in and see for yourself. All we request is that you abide by the rules. The hard work and effort to make the library a success goes to Ed Traygar, Chief Librarian, and his staff, who have contributed all their time and spirit to make the library what it is.

Staff:
Edward Trygar, Librarian
Robert Todewald
Ivan Russell
Francis T. Gorski
Theodore Wisniewski
Frank Bessone

Hobby Corner
by Bill Freund

The idea of this department is to decrease the ranks of the "Stalag-Happy" boys by introducing a new and mutual interest among the men confined here. With a little cooperation and understanding, we could help remedy this ailment. Lack of equipment should be overcome by the enthusiasm of the men to do something for themselves and their hobbies. True, most of the hobbies will be by proxy (better known as "dry-run"). To stimulate interest this writer intends to sponsor a chess and checker tournament and pick out by elimination a Compound Champ for each. Tournament rules will be observed among all contestants. A list for each will be drawn up and posted in all barracks. First, we will have Barracks eliminations to get a champ for each Barracks—to be announced in this column. And, if the "Dry-Run" Hobbyists will have patience, I expect to have something for them in the next issue.

On the Ball
by Joe Bush

June 21st, first day of summer and also the opening day of the new HAUDEGAN and MACHORKOW LEAGUES. The first game got underway at 1:30 p.m. The INDIANS of Barracks 20A defeated the SHARPS of 20B by a 7 to 1 count. Bennett pitched beautiful ball for the winners. He was robbed of a shutout by a home run in the last of the seventh inning. A big hand for the winning team. We'll have to watch them from now on.

Music Notes
by George Strawser

This department welcomes writings of musical interest. Let's have some manuscripts on music lore, fellow music lovers. Also, it is note-worthy that several Lager musicians and poets have already merged in a combination of talents toward song-writing, both classic and modern. Let's bring more of this out.

And, TRY A SONG A DAY. It helps!

LAGER GELD

The Geneva Convention mandated that prisoners of war be paid in some kind of script if forced to work. This *Lager Geld* (camp money) could be redeemed at the camp commissary for a variety of personal items.

POSTCARDS

Angelo Spinelli sent the postcards on the next two pages to his mother and brother respectively. The stamp in the upper left corner, *Geprüft*, means that the postcard had been examined by German officials. Notice the text on both cards in which Spinelli pleads for tobacco, even telling his brother, "Please, Joe, send cigarettes and good tobacco. My habits haven't changed—smoke like the dickens." The nonsmoking Spinelli, of course, wanted these tobacco products exclusively for trading purposes.

Kriegsgefangenenpost

Postkarte

An _____

Mr. Joseph Spinelli

Gebührenfrei!

Absender:

Vor- und Zuname:

G* Angelo M Spinelli

Gefangenennummer: VIIA-90199

Lager-Bezeichnung:

M.-Stammlager III B

Stalag-IIIB-200089/253

Deutschland (Allemagne)

Empfangsort: Bronx N.Y.C. New York

Straße: 1180 Lake wood Place

Land: United States of America

Landesteil (Provinz usw.

10851
U.S. CENSOR

20.8.43.-

Kriegsgefangenenlager

Datum: Aug. 15, 1943

Dear Joe:-

How are things with you Joe, Sorry Joe, that I
I always ask you for some thing whenever I write,
For there isn't any other person I can ask and trust
but you.- Please Joe, send cigarettes and good tobacco
my habits haven't changed.- Smoke like the dickens.
Send good cards, several pounds of brown and black
Coffee, tea. Use your own judgement. Love Angelo

192

Postkarte

STALAG III B · GEPRÜFT · 53

11.7.44

Mrs Domenica Spinelli

Gebührenfrei!

Absender:

Vor- und Zuname:
Sgt Angelo M. Spinelli

Gefangenennummer: III B - 90199

Lager-Bezeichnung:
M.-Stammlager III B
Stalag III B - 200089
Deutschland (Allemagne)

1035 U.S. CENSOR

Empfangsort: Bronx, N.Y.C., New York

Straße: 1180 Lakewood Place

Land: United States of America
Landesteil (Provinz usw.)

Kriegsgefangenenlager

Datum: January 1st, 44

Dear Folks:—
Christmas and New Years has come and gone. Still find myself in Germany, I'm well but homesick. Did you recieve my Dec. 26th letter. Please let me know all date of letters. Please mother send all tobacco; Half and Half, and as many boxes of cigars as possible, besides cigarettes. Hoping you'll get this card before Easter,—for I wish you all, brother Joe, Aunt Palma, Uncle Nick, Fiancée Anna & Mother, a Joyeous Easter
Your loving son - Angelo.

A LETTER HOME

In the letter opposite, Angelo Spinelli again pleads for tobacco, but he also makes it clear how important letters from home are to lonely POWs.

September 11, 1943

Dear Folks:-

At Last! Thank Heavens.- Recieved your June 10th letter on September 8th. Enjoyed reading it although it was brief.- Why not write longer ones please.? Recieved two parcels with all its contents.- Cigarettes on August 27, other on September 3rd. The clothing and the Food is very useful. The cigarettes were a blessing, especially when I'm a heavy smoker. Surprising, but many Fellows' recieve letters five to eight pages and recieve them often. Why can I? I'm in good health and kinda happy, but would enjoy being home. No need in asking for any special article, for I have mentioned them over and over again in preceeding letters. When writing to me mention dates of all letters. How are things back home. How is Joe? where is Joe, Is he that busy that he can't write at least two

letters a week. Why did'nt mother sign the letter I recieved? Give my regards to who ever asks for me, you can ask them to drop me a letter although I may not be able to answer them.- Sending all my love to mother, Joe, Aunt Palma, Uncle Nick and Anna of course - I'll be coming home someday. Love

Angelo

PACKAGES FROM HOME

Angelo Spinelli kept a notebook in which he meticulously listed everything he received while a prisoner in Stalag IIIB, including food packages, letters from home, phonograph records, and books from the International Red Cross. Most food items were consumed by Spinelli himself, but he was not above trading specific items for something else he needed.

PACKAGE FROM HOME, NO DATE

1. One lb. of Modaglia D'Oro Rice
2. One Nestles can of dried tomatoes
3. One Nestles can of granulated cheese
4. Tuaonni
5. Two boxes of chocolate snaps
6. One lb. of elbows
7. ¼ lb. of black coffee
8. ½ lb. of Borden's cheese
9. 4½ oz. of Hershey's chocolate
10. Seven packages of chicken noodle soup
11. Three packages of pea soup
12. Salami (small piece)
13. Small package of Domino Dots, 1⅝ oz
14. Eleven packages of gum
15. 100 tea balls
16. One spool of brown thread
17. One sewing kit
18. One package of pinochle cards
19. Two #2 pencils
20. One pipe
21. Two packages of pipe cleaners
22. Two cannon wash cloths
23. Two face towels
24. One 8 oz. Box of Baker's Cocoa
25. Two boxes of pipe filters
26. One tobacco pouch
27. One box of chess pieces
28. One 4 oz. package of banana flakes

PACKAGE FROM HOME, JULY 20, 1944

1. One lb. Pure Egg Dainties (Ronzoni)
2. One lb. Spaghettini (La Rosa)
3. One lb. Rice (Pastene)
4. One lb. Smith's Split Peas
5. Six oz. of pre-cooked beans (Van Camp's)
6. One lb. Egidio chocolate
7. ¼ lb. of black coffee
8. Three lollipops
9. One Lux toilet soap
10. Garlic seasoning
11. Parsley seasoning
12. Onion seasoning
13. Three boxes of tea (White Rose)
14. Eight tea balls (Your Love–White Rose)
15. Gold Tip Gum–20 packages–Fruit Flavor
16. Two packages of hot chocolate
17. Two packages of potato soup
18. Two packages of grated cheese
19. Four packages of chicken noodle soup
20. Three packages of pea soup

PACKAGE FROM HOME, AUGUST 13, 1944

1. Six boxes of La Rosa Spagettini (1 lb.)
2. One box of Smith's Split Peas
3. One box of Ronzoni Tubettini (1 lb.)
4. Six boxes of Pastina (Ronzoni) (12 oz)
5. Six boxes of Pastene Rice (1 lb.)
6. One box of Van Camps Pre-Cooked Beans
7. ½ lb. of Borden's Processed Cheese (damaged)
8. One lb. of Egidio Chocolate
9. Twenty packages of Beech Nut Gum (Spearmint)
10. Three packages of Tetley's Chicken Noodle Soup
11. One package of Lipton's Pea Soup (4 oz.)
12. Two packages of Aunt Polly's Yankee Bean Soup
13. One package of Aunt Polly's Beef Soup
14. Four packages of White Rose Tea (1 oz.)
15. Two bars of Palmolive soap
16. One lb. of Domino Dots

FORTY-SIX PHONOGRAPH RECORDS ANGELO SPINELLI RECEIVED FROM THE INTERNATIONAL RED CROSS

Angelo Spinelli wrote letters to the International Red Cross in Geneva, Switzerland, requesting phonograph records and to the YMCA asking for a record player. The International Red Cross sent him forty-six records, with at least two songs on each record. The YMCA then shipped him a hand-crank Victrola and 1,000 phonograph needles.

1. *I Love You Too Much* and *Helena*
2. *Pistol Packin' Mama* and *Wilber Force Get Off that Horse*
3. *East of the Rockies* and *When Johnny Comes Marching Home Again*
4. *Emperor Waltz* and *Southern Roses*
5. *My Own* and *Les Filles de Cadiz*
6. *Meet Me Tonight in Dreamland* and *Asleep in the Deep*
7. *Cherokee* and *A Man and His Drum*
8. *Gin Mill Blues* and *Boogie Woogie Maxine*
9. *Wine, Women and Song* and *Viennese Bonbons*
10. *Flight of the Bumble Bee* and *Push in Upper Sandusky*
11. *I'm an Old Cow Hand* and *My Little Buckaroo*
12. *Get Happy* and *Indiana*
13. *Temptation* and *I Can't Get Started*
14. *Santa Claus Is Coming to Town* and *Jingle Bells*
15. *Clementine* and *Little Ah Sid* and *Good Bye* and *Old Paint* (four songs)
16. *Il Bacio* and *Someone to Care for Me*
17. *Home Sweet Home* and *Happy Birthday* and *Auld Lang Syne* (three songs)
18. *Mexicali Rose* and *Silver on the Sage*

19. *Shoo-Shoo Baby* and *Down in the Valley*
20. *Empty Saddles* and *Round-Up Lullaby*
21. *Yancey Special* and *Celeste Blues*
22. *Boogie Woogie* and *Yancey Special*
23. *Missouri Waltz* and *Home on the Range*
24. *I Don't Want Anybody At All* and *That Old Black Magic*
25. *Casbah Blues* and *Farwell Blues*
26. *Knock Knee Sal* and *If I Didn't Care*
27. *McNamara's Band* and *She Lived Next Door to a Firehouse*
28. *Boots and Saddle* and *Twilight on the Trail*
29. *It Can't Be Wrong* and *In My Arms*
30. *I'll Be Home for Christmas* and *Danny Boy*
31. *Beer Barrel Polka* and *The New Okey Dokey Polka*
32. *Song of the Islands* and *Aloha Oe*
33. *Swamp Fire* and *Rigmarole*
34. *No Letter Today* and *I Walk Alone*
35. *When the Bloom Is on the Sage* and *It's a Lonely Trail*
36. *If I Had You* and *Smoke Gets in Your Eyes*
37. *Can't Yo' Heah Me Callin' Caroline* and *Love's Old Sweet Song*
38. *Emperor Waltz* and *Southern Roses*
39. *Sweet Leilani* and *Blue Hawaii*
40. *Reverie* and *Golliwog's Cakewalk*
41. *No Name Jive*, Parts 1 & 2
42. *Tales from the Vienna Woods* and *Emperor Waltz*
43. *Song of India* and *Alice Blue Gown*
44. *A Blues Serenade* and *S'posin'*
45. *Dusk in Upper Sandusky* and *Flight of the Bumble Bee*
46. *I Wonder What's Become of Sally* and *Darling, Je Vous Aime Beaucoup*

BOOKS AND MAGAZINES ANGELO SPINELLI RECEIVED FROM THE INTERNATIONAL RED CROSS

The irrepressible Angelo Spinelli also managed to convince the International Red Cross to send him a wide variety of books and magazines. In addition, Spinelli asked Col. Darryl Zanuck, whom he had met in North Africa, to ship him a book, which the Hollywood producer did through Harrods of London. Spinelli donated all his books and magazines to the camp library in Stalag IIIB. As he did with all received items, Spinelli wrote down the titles of the books and magazines in his notebook.

1. *The Amateur Photographer*, 6 issues: July 28, Aug. 11, Aug. 18, Aug. 24, Sept. 1, and Sept. 8, 1944.
2. *Cine Kodak* Magazines, 9 Issues: Dec. 1936; May, Sept.–Oct., Nov.–Dec. 1937; March 1937; April–May, Sept.–Oct., Nov.–Dec., 1938; March–April 1939.
3. C. H. Grandgent and E. H. Wilkins, *Italian Grammar*.
4. C. M. Sauer and Pietro Mott, *Italian Conversation and Grammar*.
5. C. R. Gibson, *How Photography Came About*.
6. Dante Alighieri, *The Divine Comedy: Inferno*, translated by H. W. Longfellow.
7. Dante Alighieri, *The Divine Comedy: The Vision of Dante Alighieri*, translated by Rev. H. F. Cary.
8. David Livingstone, *Missionary Travels and Researches in South Africa*.
9. Dr. T. Gerald Garry, *African Doctor*.
10. Emory S. Bogardus, *Sociology*.

11. H. B. Cotterill, *L'Inferno di Dante*. Bilingual Series.
12. L. A. G. Strong, *The Director* (first edition—sent by Harrods of London).
13. Larry June, *The Photographer's Rule Book*.
14. Lucia Moholy, *A Hundred Years of Photography*.
15. R. D. Carmichael, J. H. Weaver, L. Lapaz, *The Calculus*.
16. S. A. Queen, *Social Work in the Light of History*.
17. Robert Taft, *Photography and the American Scene*.
18. Vida D. Scudder, *Socialism and Character*.

NOTES

INTRODUCTION

1. C. Ross Greening and Angelo Spinelli, in collaboration with John R. Burkhart. *The Yankee Kriegies: How Our POWs Made "Little Americas" Behind Nazi Barbed Wire* (New York: National Council of Young Men's Christian Associations, 1946).

2. Lewis H. Carlson, *We Were Each Other's Prisoners: An Oral History of World War II American and German Prisoners of War* (New York: Basic Books, 1997).

3. To his credit, Tom Brokaw does include several former POWs in his *The Greatest Generation* (New York: Random House, 1998), as well as in his *An Album of Memories: Personal Histories from the Greatest Generation* (New York: Random House, 2001).

4. F. W. Von Fricken, a German officer in Stalag IIIB, reported these statistics in a draft of an article he hoped to publish entitled "The Memorable Memorial Day of 1943," a copy of which he gave Spinelli in 1986 when they resumed their prison-camp friendship at a meeting in New Jersey.

5. Quoted in Linda Puner, "Picturing POW Camp Life," *Gannett Westchester Rockland Newspapers* (July 8, 1990), 9.

6. Most of this background information on Stalag IIIB is from a U.S. War Department Military Intelligence Service Report, dated November 1, 1945, which itself was based on interviews with former prisoners and reports from U.S. military intelligence, the International Red Cross, and German military officials.

7. Tim Wolter, *POW Baseball in World War II: The National Pastime Behind Barbed Wire* (Jefferson, N.C.: McFarland and Co., 2002), 66.

8. Certainly not all German officials were so diligent in implementing the Geneva Accord's stipulations for the treatment of POWs. According to fellow officer F. W. Von Fricken, Blau had been ordered to make Stalag IIIB "internationally known, specifically among neutrals, for the strictest adherence to the articles set forth in the Geneva Convention [and] to create a favorable impression in regards to the humane treatment among the inmates." Von Fricken admitted, "The Russian prisoners of war, of course, were exempt since their government did not recognize this Convention"; F. W. Von Fricken, "The Memorable Memorial Day of 1943," unpublished essay, n.d.

9. Letter from Von Fricken to Spinelli, January 2, 1982.

10. Letter from Von Fricken to Spinelli, December 16, 1991.

11. One of the worst violations of the Geneva Accord occurred in Stalag IXB, an enlisted men's camp at Bad Orb, where the German *Kommandant* singled out Jewish-American POWs (they had an "H" on their dog tags) and sent them to a slave labor camp at Berga where approximately 20 percent of the 350 Americans died. See Carlson, *We Were Each Other's Prisoners*, 194–99 and Mitchell G. Bard, *Forgotten Victims: The Abandonment of Americans in Hitler's Camps* (Boulder, Colo.: Westview Press, 1994).

12. The 1929 Geneva Accord was very conscious of the benefits of class. Prisoners were segregated according to rank, with separate camps for officers, noncommissioned officers, and enlisted men. Germany also set aside special camps for U.S. Air Corps prisoners that were administered by Hermann Goering's *Luftwaffe*. Officers and NCOs could not be required to work, although NCOs could volunteer to do so. Enlisted men had no choice in the matter. Similarly, the

Geneva Accord defined the area and quality of living space according to rank. Officers usually enjoyed better food, and the highest-ranking officers were entitled to orderlies and aides-de-camp who were expected to make their superiors' beds, wash their clothes, and perform necessary duties around the camp, including cleaning the officers' latrines.

13. Such inspections usually occurred at three-month intervals during which the International Red Cross inspectors were always accompanied by officials of the German government.

14. Jack T. Sneesby, unpublished memoir, n.d. Sneesby points out that this loss of extra clothing later caused problems, especially after large numbers of ill-clad new prisoners poured into IIIB during and after the Battle of the Bulge.

15. Quoted in Greening and Spinelli, *The Yankee Kriegies*, 33. Those signing were Brig. Gen. Arthur W. Vanaman, Cols. Darr H. Alkire, Delmar T. Spivey, Jean R. Byerly, A. Y. Smith, Charles G. Goodrich, Daniel W. Jenkins, and Einar A. Malmstrom, and Lt. Col. Francis S. Gabreski.

16. One American prisoner who took advantage of these educational opportunities was future Attorney General Nicholas Katzenbach who while a prisoner in Stalag Luft III completed much of his work for his subsequent law degree; see Arthur A. Durand, *Stalag Luft III: the Secret Story* (Baton Rouge: Louisiana University Press, 1988), 226.

17. The YMCA should not be blamed for the disparity in who received and enjoyed these many items. All were distributed by the International Red Cross, which itself was extremely class-conscious and much more committed to the welfare of officers than of the lower ranks. In addition, during the early years of the war, when Germany was rolling up its initial victories, the International Red Cross was very solicitous of German interests.

18. One could find clandestine radios, constructed by the prisoners themselves or smuggled in, in nearly all German prison camps.

19. Sneesby, unpublished memoir.

20. Although the term "post-traumatic stress disorder" did not come into use until

the 1980s, a recent British study suggests that 90 percent of prisoners in World War II suffered its effects.

21. See Carlson, *We Were Each Other's Prisoners*, 73.

22. Durand, *Stalag Luft III*, 346.

23. Shortly after the end of the war, Swiss Radio confirmed that Dr. Burckhardt, President of the International Red Cross, which was based in Switzerland, had learned of a possible execution order. As a result, in March 1945 Burckhardt met with representatives of Himmler and obtained permission for the International Red Cross to enter the prison camps in the final weeks of the war to prevent any last-minute executions.

24. For the prisoners interned in Poland, these marches lasted for weeks and sometimes covered more than 300 miles during what was considered the worst winter of the century. Predictably, many of these men did not survive, especially if they had to walk the entire distance.

25. Carlson, *We Were Each Other's Prisoners*, 93–94.

26. Sneesby, unpublished memoir.

27. Carlson, *We Were Each Other's Prisoners*, 180–81.

28. Carlson, *We Were Each Other's Prisoners*, 94.

29. Bill Hendrick, "I Was Told to Take Pictures, and I Did," *Atlanta Journal Constitution*, April 7, 2000.

30. Eric Reinert, "POW Photos Donated to Andersonville National Historic Site," *Cultural Resource Management*, No. 56 (2000), 65.

31. Letter from Joe DiMare to Spinelli, undated.

32. Letter to Sen. Connie Mack from Lt. Col. Leland W. Klein, U.S. Army Congressional Coordinator, Office of the Secretary of the Army, June 5, 1989.

ANGELO SPINELLI'S NARRATIVE

1. The Allied prisoners referred to themselves as "Kriegies," slang for the German word *Kriegsgefangenen*, which translates as "prisoners of war."

2. "Yank, Axis Prisoner, Greets His Family in N.Y. by Radio," New York *Daily News,* March 4, 1943, 2.

3. SS was short for *Schutzstaffel* which, literally translated, means "Protection Squadrons." Usually hated, and always feared, the SS under Heinrich Himmler became the security arm of the Nazi Party and the perpetrator of some of the worst domestic and military atrocities of the Third Reich, including the administration of the concentration camps and the organization of the "final solution" in 1941. In the final year of the war the SS moved to take over the POW camps from the Wehrmacht, especially after the Great Escape of March 24, 1944.

4. According to historian Arthur A. Durand's *Stalag Luft III*, 89, the term "goon" stemmed from a comic strip in the London *Daily Mirror* "that depicted 'goons' as low-browed, primitive apemen of great strength and stupidity." The American soldiers also referred to Germans as "krauts," which was a derisive reference to sauerkraut.

5. The *POW-WOW* was usually four pages long and handwritten. This editorial was from the first issue, dated June 25, 1943, and was given to Spinelli after the war by F. W. Von Fricken. It was likely written by Frank Stebbing, the editor-in-chief, or by "Pop" Dimmick, who was the associate editor. The original of this issue of the *POW-WOW* is now in the Yale University Archives *(see Appendix, pp. 182–89).*

6. Von Fricken, "The Memorable Memorial Day of 1943."

7. Red Cross parcels differed, depending on when they were put together and by which Allied country. An early American-packed A-1 Box might include two cans of coffee, liver pâté, corned beef, cocoa, sugar, powdered milk, a Class D bar, hard candy, two packages of cigarettes, matches, dried biscuits, raisins, and cheese. A U.S. No. 9 Box might include three packs of cigarettes, two boxes of powdered orange drink, coffee, one box of sugar cubes, five meats, one cheese, powdered milk, and cookies. Some of the later parcels included gloves, socks, sweaters, handkerchiefs, soap, sewing kits, shaving soap, razor blades, and a toothbrush and paste.

8. One such Russian in Stalag IIIB was Dr. Nikita Zakaravich Asseyev, a dentist who insisted he and hundreds of other Russian prisoners owed their lives to American prisoners who risked their lives to throw food over the fence into their compound. Asseyev's story was first told by Robert L. Taylor for the Russian-language magazine *America Illustrated* ("Life and Death In Stalag IIIB," February 1989). It was then retold in Charles Kuralt's *A Life on the Road* (New York: G. P. Putnam's Sons, 1990) and condensed for *Reader's Digest* as "The Russian Who Never Forgot" (November 1990), 132–36. Several of Spinelli's photographs appear in these articles.

9. Spinelli also requested and received a phonograph, records, and 1,000 needles from the YMCA *(see Appendix, p. 198–9).*

10. Again, officer and NCO camps were much more likely to receive recreational equipment than were those camps holding enlisted men.

11. F. W. Von Fricken also remembers this incident with the baseball: In a January 2, 1982, letter to Spinelli, Von Fricken wrote, "If I am not mistaken, it was you who one day tried to retrieve a baseball which had rolled into the No-Man's Land. A Tower guard instantly opened fire and as a result you could proudly afterwards show off a bullet hole at the lower part of your pants. For quite a while you stayed away from that dangerous zone and concentrated on your bartering, in which you had no equal."

12. Frank Stebbing first published this poem in Stalag IIIB's *POW-WOW*. After the war it was reprinted in Greening and Spinelli's *The Yankee Kriegies*, 20.

13. The Geneva Accord mandated a minimum payment for POWs who were forced to work. This script could be used to purchase items in a camp store called a Kantine *(see photo, p. 163 and Appendix, p. 190).*

14. Interview with La Porta, October 18, 2001.

15. Letter from DiMare to Spinelli, n. d.

16. Interview with Parrott, November 19, 2001.

17. The Germans also stamped Geprüft on outgoing mail *(see Appendix, p. 192–3).*

18. Interview with La Porta, October 18, 2001.

19. The photographs Spinelli took with this Robat camera are also in Andersonville, as is the camera itself.
20. As mentioned in the introduction, shortly before ending his own life, Hitler allegedly ordered the execution of all prisoners. Although this final command was never implemented, such rumors abounded in the prison camps. For example, Richard Varley, who, like Angelo Spinelli, was incarcerated in Stalag IIIB, heard a rumor that Hitler had promised to make the prisoners "pay the supreme penalty for the deadly air raids by the Luftgangsters," as the Germans called the Allied bombers and their pilots; unpublished World War II Diary of Richard K. Varley, p. 30. Copies of Varley's diary are in the Iowa Gold Star Museum, Johnston, Iowa, and in the POW Museum at the Andersonville National Historic Site, Andersonville, Georgia.

BIBLIOGRAPHY

WORLD WAR II GERMAN-HELD AMERICAN POWS: MONOGRAPHS AND NONFICTION

Bard, Mitchell G. *Forgotten Victims: The Abandonment of Americans in Hitler's Camps.* Boulder, Colo.: Westview Press, 1994.

Barker, A. J. *Prisoners of War.* New York: Universe Books, 1975.

Baron, Richard, Abe Baum, and Richard Goldhurst. *Raid! The Untold Story of Patton's Secret Mission.* New York: G. P. Putnam's Sons, 1981.

Brickhill, Paul. *The Great Escape.* New York: W. W. Norton and Co., 1950.

Burgess, Alan. *The Longest Tunnel: The True Story of World War II's Great Escape.* New York: Grove Weidenfeld, 1990.

Cohen, Bernard M., and Maurice Z. Cooper. *A Follow-Up Study of World War II Prisoners of War.* Washington, D.C.: U.S. Government Printing Office, 1954.

Doyle, Robert C. *A Prisoner's Duty: Great Escapes in U.S. Military History.* Annapolis: Naval Institute Press, 1997.

———. *Voices from Captivity: Interpreting the American POW Narrative.* Lawrence: University Press of Kansas, 1994.

Durand, Arthur A. *Stalag Luft III: The Secret Story.* Baton Rouge: Louisiana State University Press, 1988.

Foy, David A. *For You the War Is Over: American Prisoners of War in Nazi Germany.* New York: Stein and Day, 1984.

Kelnhofer, Guy J. *Life after Liberation: Understanding the Former Prisoner of War.* Essays. St. Paul, Minn.: Banfil Street Press, 1992.

Moore, Bob, and Kent Fedorowich, eds. *Prisoners of War and Their Captors in World War II.* Oxford: Berg, 1996.

Shoemaker, Lloyd R. *The Escape Factory: The Story of MIS-X.* New York: St. Martin's Press, 1990.

Trials of War Criminals Before the Nuremberg Military Tribunals. vols. 11 and 13. Washington, D.C.: U.S. Government Printing Office, 1952.

Vulliet, Andre. *The YMCA and Prisoners of War During World War II.* Geneva: International Committee of the YMCA, 1946.

Weingartner, James. *Crossroads of Death: The Story of the Malmédy Massacre and Trial.* Berkeley: University of California Press, 1979.

Wolter, Tim. *POW Baseball in World War II: The National Pastime Behind Barbed Wire.* Jefferson, N.C.: McFarland and Co., 2002.

MEMOIRS, BIOGRAPHIES, AND ORAL HISTORIES

Abdalla, John. *Allen King, World War II American P.O.W.* Memphis: Oral History Research Office, Memphis State University, 1989.

Beattie, Edward W. *Diary of a Kriegie.* New York: Thomas Crowell Co., 1946.

Beltrone, Art and Lee. *A Wartime Log.* Charlottesville, Va.: Howell Press, 1995.

Bing, Richard L. *You're 19 . . . Welcome Home: A Study of the Air War Over Europe and Its After Effects.* Self-published, 1992.

Bird, Tom. *American POWs of World War II: Forgotten Men Tell Their Stories.* Westport, Conn.: Praeger, 1993.

Brokaw, Tom. *An Album of Memories: Personal Histories from the Greatest Generation.* New York: Random House, 2001.

———. *The Greatest Generation.* New York: Random House, 1998.

Carlson, Lewis H. *We Were Each Other's Prisoners: An Oral History of World War II American and German Prisoners of War.* New York: Basic Books, 1997.

Carpenter, Willis and Roberta. *I Was the Enemy.* Millersburg, Ind.: Privately printed, 1990.

Chernitsky, Dorothy. *Voices from the Foxholes: Men of the 110th Infantry Relate Personal Accounts of What They Experienced During World War II.* Uniontown, Pa.: Privately printed, 1991.

Chiesl, O. M. *Clipped Wings.* Dayton, Ohio: R. W. Kimball, 1948.

Collins, Douglas. *POW.* New York: W. W. Norton and Co., 1968.

Cox, Luther. *Always Fighting the Enemy.* Baltimore: Gateway Press, 1990.

Crosby, Donald F., SJ. *Battlefield Chaplains: Catholic Priests in World War II.* Lawrence: University Press of Kansas, 1994.

Daniel, Eugene L. *In the Presence of Mine Enemies: An American Chaplain in World War II German Prison Camps.* Charlotte, N.C.: E. L. Daniel, Jr., 1985.

David, Clayton C. *They Helped Me Escape: From Amsterdam to Gibraltar in 1944.* Manhattan, Kans.: Sunflower University Press, 1988.

Davis, George J. *The Hitler Diet, As Inflicted on American P.O.W.'s in World War II.* Los Angeles: Military Literary Guild, 1990.

Dillon, Carrol F. *A Domain of Heroes: An Airman's Life Behind Barbed Wire in Germany in World War II.* Sarasota Fla.: Palm Island Press, 1995.

Dobran, Edward A. *P.O.W.* New York: Exposition Press, 1953.

Dolph, Harry A. *The Evader.* Austin, Tex.: Eakin Press, 1991.

Duke, Florimond. *Name, Rank, and Serial Number.* New York: Meredith Press, 1969.

Ferguson, Clarence. *Kriegsgefangener 3074, Prisoner of War.* Waco, Tex.: Texian Press, 1983.

Fisher, Charles A. *Mission Number Three: Missing in Action.* Latrobe, Pa.: St. Vincent College, Center for Northern Appalachian Studies, 1998.

Frelinghuysen, Joseph S. *Passages to Freedom.* Manhattan, Kans.: Sunflower University Press, 1990.

Halmos, Eugene E. *The Wrong Side of the Fence: A United States Army Air Corps POW in World War II*. Shippensburg, Pa.: White Mane, 1996.

Hamann, Lorin W. *A Prisoner Remembers World War II*. Elkader, Iowa: Self-published, 1984.

Harrison, Jack S. *Flight from Youth: The Story of an American POW*. Madison, Wis.: J. S. Harrison, 1973.

Harsh, George. *Lonesome Road*. New York: W. W. Norton and Co., 1971.

Hatch, Gardner, John S. Edwards, et al., eds. *American Ex-Prisoners of War*. 4 Volumes. Paducah, Ky.: Turner Publishers, 1988, 1991.

Higgins, Samuel G. *Survival: The Diary of an American POW in World War II*. Central Point, Ore.: Hellgate Press, n.d.

Hopewell, Clifford. *Combine 13*. Dallas: Merrimore Press, 1990.

Howell, Forrest W. *Whispers of Death: Yankee Kriegies*. Moore Haven, Fla.: Rainbow Books, 1985.

Jackson, Robert L. *Kriegie: Prisoner of War*. Buchanan, Mich.: Self-published, 1997.

Kaufman, Henry. *Vertrauensmann: Man of Confidence: The Story of an American Ex-Prisoner of World War II*. New York: Rivercross Publishing, 1994.

Lister, Hal. *Krautland Calling: An American POW Radio Broadcaster in Nazi Germany*. Austin, Tex.: Eakin Press, 1989.

Maher, William P. *Fated to Survive*. Spartanburg, S.C.: Honoribus Press, 1992.

McBride, Charles C. *Mission Failure and Survival*. Manhattan, Kans.: Sunflower University Press, 1989.

McCullen, Dan. *Lest We Forget: A POW Memoir of World War II*. Santa Barbara, Calif.: Fithian Press, 1997.

Meltesen, Clarence R. *Roads to Liberation from Oflag 64*. San Francisco: Oflag 64 Press, 1990.

Moramarco, Nick. *Missing in Action*. Santa Barbara, Calif.: Fithian Press, 1999.

Neary, Robert P. *Stalag Luft III*. Strasburg, Pa.: 8th Air Force Association reprint, 1992.

Newcomb, Alan. *Vacation with Pay: Being an Account of My Stay at the German Rest

Camp for Tired Allied Airmen at Beautiful Barth-on-the-Baltic (Stalag Luft 1). Haverhill, Mass.: Destiny Publishers, 1947.

O'Donnell, Joseph P. *Luftgangsters*. Robbinsville, N.J.: Self-published, 1982.

———. *The Shoe Leather Express: The Evacuation of Kriegsgefangener Lager Stalag Luft IV, Deutschland, Germany*. Robbinsville, N.J.: Self-published, 1982.

Richard, Oscar G. III. *Kriegie: An American POW in Germany*. Baton Rouge: Louisiana State University Press, 2000.

Sage, Col. Jerry. *Sage: The Man the Germans Could Not Keep Prisoner*. Wayne, Pa.: Miles Standish Press, 1985.

Sampson, Francis. *Paratrooper Padre*. Washington, D.C.: Catholic University of America Press, 1948.

Sexton, Winton K. *Back Roads to Freedom*. Kansas City, Mo.: Lowell Press, 1985.

Simmons, Kenneth W. *Kriegie*. New York: Thomas Nelson and Sons, 1960.

Spiller, Harry. *Prisoners of Nazis: Accounts by American POWs in World War II*. Jefferson, N.C.: McFarland, 1998.

Spivey, Delmar T. *POW Odyssey: Recollections of Center Compound, Stalag Luft III and the Secret German Peace Mission in World War II*. Attleboro, Mass.: Colonial Lithograph, 1984.

Stone, James F. *A Holiday in Hitlerland*. New York: Carlton Press, 1970.

TenHaken, Mel. *Bail Out! POW 1944–1945*. Manhattan, Kans.: Sunflower University Press, 1990.

Terkel, Studs. *The Good War: An Oral History of World War II*. New York: Pantheon Books, 1984.

Tyler, Leslie J. *Wild Blue Yonder: An Adventure of Hitler's Hostages*. Grawn, Mich.: Crystal Publishing, 1992.

Victor, John A. *Time Out: American Airmen at Stalag Luft 1*. Fallbrook, Calif.: Aero Publications, 1984.

Westheimer, David. *Sitting It Out: A World War II POW Memoir*. Houston: Rice University Press, 1992.

Weymouth, Major Guy. *A.W.O.L.* London: Tom Donovan, 1993.

Worley, Robert. *Don't Fence Me In.* Tucson, Ariz.: Self-published, 1993.

Worthen, Frederick D. *Against All Odds: Surviving World War II.* Santa Barbara, Calif.: Fithian Press, 1996.

Zemke, Hubert. *Zemke's Stalag: The Final Days of World War II.* Washington, D.C.: Smithsonian Institution Press, 1991.

———. *Zemke's Wolf Pack: The Story of Hub Zemke and the 56th Fighter Group in the Skies Over Europe.* New York: Orion Books, 1989.

NOVELS ABOUT AMERICAN POWS IN WORLD WAR II GERMANY

Giovannitti, Len. *The Prisoners of Combine D.* New York: Bantam Books, 1957.

Klaas, Joe. *Maybe I'm Dead.* New York: Henry Holt, 1955.

Vonnegut, Kurt. *Slaughterhouse-Five or the Children's Crusade, a Duty-Dance with Death.* New York: Delacorte Press, 1969.

Westheimer, David. *Song of the Young Sentry.* Boston: Little, Brown, 1968.

———. *Von Ryan's Express.* Garden City, N.Y.: Doubleday, 1964.

UNPUBLISHED M.A. THESES

Burbank, Lyman B. "A History of the American Air Force Prisoners of War in Center Compound, Stalag Luft II, Germany." M.A. Thesis, University of Chicago, 1946.

Goldman, Ben. "German Treatment of American Prisoners of War in World War II." M.A. Thesis, Wayne State University, 1949.

DOCUMENTARY FILMS FEATURING GERMAN-HELD AMERICAN POWS

Behind the Lines: World War II: Fields of Play, Fields of Battle. ESPN, December 7, 2001.

Oflag 64: A POW Odyssey. PBS, February 20, 2002.

P.O.W.: Americans in Enemy Hands: World War II, Korea, and Vietnam. Arnold Shapiro Productions, 1987.

POWs Who Were Left Behind. ABC, September 11, 1992.

FEATURE FILMS FEATURING GERMAN-HELD AMERICAN POWS

The Colditz Story. British Lion, 1957.

Escape to Athena. ITC, 1979.

The Great Escape. Mirisch, 1963.

Hart's War. MGM, 2002.

The Secret War of Henry Frigg. Universal, 1968.

Slaughterhouse-Five. Universal, 1972.

Stalag 17. Paramount, 1953.

Victory. Lorimar, 1981.

Von Ryan's Express. 20th Century Fox, 1965.

BOOKS CONTAINING SPINELLI PHOTOGRAPHS AND BIOGRAPHICAL MATERIALS

Bailey, Ronald H., and the editors of Time-Life Books. *Prisoners of World War II*. Alexandria, Va.: Time-Life Books, 1981 (14 photos).

Carlson, Lewis H. *We Were Each Other's Prisoners: An Oral History of World War II American and German Prisoners of War*. New York: Basic Books, 1997 (1 photo).

Greening, C. Ross, and Angelo Spinelli, in collaboration with John R. Burkhart. *The Yankee Kriegies: How Our POWs Made "Little Americas" Behind Nazi Barbed Wire*. New York: National Council of Young Men's Christian Associations, 1946 (26 photos).

Hatch, Gardner. *The American Prisoner of War*. Paducah, Ky.: Turner Publishing Co., 1987 (9 photos).

Kuralt, Charles. *Life on the Road*. New York: G. P. Putnam's Sons, 1990.

Marsh, Alan, Eric Reinert, and Fred Sanchez. *Spinelli: Behind the Wire. Prisoner of War Images by Angelo Spinelli. A Photographic Exhibit by Andersonville National Historic Site*. Andersonville, Ga.: The Friends of Andersonville, 2000 (92 photos).

Taylor, Thomas H. *The Simple Sounds of Freedom*. New York: Random House, 2002 (1 photo).

Wolter, Tim. *POW Baseball in World War II: The National Pastime Behind Barbed Wire*. Jefferson, N.C.: McFarland and Co., 2001 (14 photos).

PERIODICALS CONTAINING SPINELLI PHOTOGRAPHS AND BIOGRAPHICAL MATERIALS

Cox, Frank. "The Secret Camera of Angelo Spinelli." *Soldiers*. April 1989, 11–12 (6 photos). This article was reprinted in the *Ex-POW Bulletin*. September 1989, 34–36. Florida Congressman Lawrence J. Smith also placed this article in the *Congressional Record*, v. 135, no. 48, E1346-7, April 25, 1989.

DiMare, Joe. "The Leaf of Gold." *EX-POW Bulletin*. August 1990, 47–48 (1 photo).

Ford, E. L. "Legion of Merit Medal Citation." *Italian American Review*. April 17, 1993, 122.

"Information." *EX-POW Bulletin*. September 1991, 27 (1 photo).

"Life as a POW." *The National Italian American Foundation News*. Winter 2002, 21 (1 photo).

O'Steen, Robert. "Faith Enabled POW to Survive, Outwit Nazis." *Florida Catholic*. July 19, 1991.

———. "The Knight Who Fooled the Nazis." *Columbia*. September 1991, 12–13 (4 photos).

Reinert, Eric. "POW Photos Donated to Andersonville National Historic Site." *Cultural Resource Management*. No. 56, July 2000, 65 (1 photo).

"The Russian Who Never Forgot." *Reader's Digest*. November 1990, 132–36.

Smith, Lawrence J. "Angelo Spinelli." *Congressional Record*. v. 135, no. 48, April 25, 1989.

Spinelli, Angelo. "The Season's Greetings." *Ex-POW Bulletin*. December 1987, 47.

Spinelli, James J. "Angelo M. Spinelli: Photographer of Freedoms Lost." *Italian American Review*. April 17, 1993, 122–29.

"Stalag IIIB." *EX-POW Bulletin*. September 1985, 22 (1 photo).

"Stalag IIIB Photographed." *EX-POW Bulletin*. August 1981, 16–23 (13 photos).

Taylor, Robert L. "Life and Death in Stalag IIIB." *America Illustrated*. February 1989. *America Illustrated* was published for distribution in the Soviet Union by the United States Information Agency (6 photos).

"This Is Our Story." *EX-POW Bulletin*. August 1972, 15.

Ward, Hiley H. "Lensman's Secret Focus in WWII." *Media History Digest*. Fall–Winter, 1989, 59–65 (5 photos). This article was reprinted in the *Ex-POW Bulletin*, August 1990, 42–46.

NEWSPAPERS CONTAINING SPINELLI PHOTOGRAPHS AND BIOGRAPHICAL MATERIALS

Berman, Herb. "Before Candid Camera . . . There was Angelo Spinelli." *VIA–The Voice of Italian American Monthly Newspaper*. March/April 1991, 10–11 (7 photos).

———. "One Picture Is Worth a Thousand Words." *VIA–The Voice of Italian American Monthly Newspaper*. April/May 1991, 15 (1 photo).

Brown, Drew. "From 'Behind the Wire': POW Museum Exhibits Photos from Prison Camp." *The Macon Telegraph*. April 8, 2000, 1, 9A (2 photos).

Conway, Caron. "Hallandale Resident Remembers 'Hell' as POW." *Hallandale Digest*. July 20, 1989, 1 (3 photos).

Hendrick, Bill. "I Was Told to Take Pictures and I Did." *Atlanta Journal Constitution*. April 7, 2000, Section E, 1 (8 photos).

———. "I Was Told to Take Pictures and I Did." *San Francisco Chronicle*. April 17, 2000, Section A, 3 (2 photos).

Heidelberg, Paul. "Images from a POW." *Fort Lauderdale News/Sun Sentinel*. January 13, 1988, 1, 12–13 (9 photos).

Hughes, Bill. "POW Life in Pictures." *The Journal News*, Westchester, N.Y. May 9, 2001, 1–2 (2 photos). Reprinted in *Ex-POW Bulletin*, August 2001, 24–25.

Jedermann, Ken. "Incredible Photographs of a 'Kriegie'." *The Stars and Stripes*. October 2, 1989, 16 (4 photos).

Kalajian, Douglas. "A POW's Scrapbook." *Miami Herald*. April 9, 1990, Section C, 1 (4 photos).

Lavigne, Regina. "The War Remembered: Photographer POW Secretly Took Photos of Nazi Camp." *Senior Life and Leisure*. April 1991, 5 (2 photos).

McDonnell, Claudia. "Record of Survival." *Catholic New York*. September 6, 1990, 36 (1 photo).

O'Steen, Robert. "Faith Enabled POW to Survive, Outwit Nazis." *The Florida Catholic.* July 19, 1991, 1, 10–12 (5 photos).

Puner, Linda. "Picturing POW Camp Life." *Gannett Westchester Rockland Newspapers.* July 8, 1990, 1, 8–9 (5 photos).

Schaffer, Kerry. "Fear Itself." *Gannett Westchester Rockland Newspapers.* July 8, 1990, 2 (7 photos).

Wiltrout, Kate. "Images of Captivity: Secret Photos of a German POW Come to Mighty Eighth." *Savannah Morning News on the Web.* July 4, 2000 (3 photos).

"Yank, Axis Prisoner, Greets His Family in N.Y. by Radio." New York *Daily News.* March 4, 1943, 2.

ARCHIVAL COLLECTIONS

Collection of Photographs, Series A–B and C–D, Yale University Manuscripts and Archives.

Laufer, Matthew I. "Sergeant Angelo Spinelli and His Photographs: Making and Collection History." Yale University, Manuscripts and Archives, December 6, 1994.

National Prisoner of War Museum, Andersonville National Historic Site, Andersonville, Georgia. This is the repository for all existing Spinelli photographic negatives, his two cameras, and his tripod.

Spinelli, Angelo. "Reminiscences: History of the Secret Camera and Its Results, Historical Significance." *Angelo Spinelli Papers*, Yale University, Manuscripts and Archives, 1992.

———. "Reminiscences: Several Anecdotes and Important Incidents." *Angelo Spinelli Papers*, Yale University, Manuscripts and Archives, 1992.

OTHER SOURCES

American Ex-Prisoners of War 2002 Engagement Calendar. Sponsored by the American Ex-Prisoners of War Organization, this calendar includes a biographical sketch of Angelo Spinelli written by Alan Marsh, the Cultural Resources Program Manager of the Andersonville National Historic Site POW Museum (14 photos).

Sneesby, Jack T. Unpublished memoir, n.d.

Varley, Richard K. *World War II Diary of Richard K. Varley*. Unpublished. Copies of Varley's diary are in the Iowa Gold Star Museum, Johnston, Iowa, and in the POW Museum at the Andersonville National Historic Site, Andersonville, Georgia.

Von Fricken, F. W. "The Memorable Memorial Day of 1943." Unpublished essay by former German officer in Stalag IIIB, given to Angelo Spinelli by Von Fricken in 1986.

TELEVISION

"Angelo's Story." WSAV Savannah, Ga., August 29, 2000.

"Cardinal John O'Connor's Solemn Pontifical Sunday Mass." December 27, 1992.

"CNN Sunday Morning: The Man and His Pictures." April 30, 2000.

"Headline News." CNN, April 30, 2000.

"Interact Atlanta: Angelo's Pictures." Channel 36, Atlanta, Ga., May 13, 2000.

"Italics: The Italian American Magazine." Channel 75, New York City, May 31, 2001.

"On the Road, with Charles Kuralt." CBS, June 17, 1988; repeated October 14, 1988.

EXHIBITS FEATURING SPINELLI PHOTOGRAPHS

"World War II: Personal Accounts—Pearl Harbor to V-J Day." National Archives Exhibit (4 photos). This exhibit showed in the following museums and presidential libraries:

San Antonio Museum of Art, San Antonio, Tex., Dec. 7, 1991, to Mar. 29, 1992

Lyndon B. Johnson Library, Austin, Tex., Apr. 18 to Aug. 23, 1992

Dwight D. Eisenhower Library, Abilene, Kans., Sept. 19, 1992, to Jan. 4, 1993

Harry S. Truman Library, Independence, Mo., Mar. 6 to August 15, 1993

Gerald R. Ford Museum, Grand Rapids, Mich., Sept. 3, 1993, to Jan. 3, 1994

Jimmy Carter Library, Atlanta, Ga. Jan. 29 to May 30, 1994

IBM Gallery of Science and Art, New York, N.Y., June 14 to August 27, 1994

John F. Kennedy Library, Boston, Mass., Sept. 24, 1994, to Jan. 2, 1995

Ronald Reagan Library, Simi Valley, Calif., Jan. 21 to April 9, 1995

National Archives, Washington, D.C., May 6 to Nov. 11, 1995

"Behind the Barbed Wire: Angelo Spinelli's Photo-Documentation on Life and Culture in a POW Stalag Camp." National Prisoner of War Museum, Andersonville Historic Site, April 2000 (92 Photos). This exhibit also traveled to the following locations:

Mighty Eighth Air Force Heritage Museum, Savannah, Ga., June 2000.

Fort Benning National Infantry Museum, Fort Benning, Ga., September 2000.

Mamaroneck Public Library, Mamaroneck, N.Y., May 2001.

Yonkers Public Library, Yonkers, N.Y., June 4 to July 31, 2001.

Georgia College and State University, Milledgeville, Ga., March 1 to May 31, 2002.

Italian American Museum, New York, N.Y. In April 2003, the exhibit became part of the museum's permanent collection.

SPECIAL CITATIONS RECOGNIZING ANGELO SPINELLI'S MILITARY AND PHOTOGRAPHIC ACHIEVEMENTS

American Ex-Prisoners of War, Certificate of Award, "In Appreciation of Outstanding Service to the Organization and Community," October 9, 1993.

Knights of Columbus, Certificate of Commendation, 3rd and 4th Degrees, September 28, 1992.

U.S. Army, Legion of Merit, "For Exceptionally Meritorious Conduct in the Performance of Outstanding Service," November 19, 1943.

INDEX

Note: Page numbers in boldface indicate a photo or illustration.